Grappling
with
Reality

By

Kevin 0'Hagan 5th Dan

Printed by
New Breed Publishing
Po box 511
Dagenham
Essex RM9 5DN

Email Marc Kaylor

mkaylor.newbreed@talk21.com

About the author

Kevin O'Hagan is a professional Martial Arts/Self Protection instructor. He has trained in the Martial Arts for some 23 years now. He holds the rank of 5th Dan black belt in 'Goshin' Ju Jutsu and 1st Dan black in Atemi Jutsu. He is one of the new breed of instructors who are teaching practical Combat Arts and also cross training principles in the UK today. He successfully runs clubs in the Bristol area and is a registered instructor with the British Combat Association, the leading lights in 'real' Self Protection today. Kevin is also a fully qualified fitness instructor and works in the gym's of the local council sports centres. He is also becoming an accomplished writer having written articles for magazines like, *'Fighters'*, *'Combat'* and *Martial Arts illustrated.'* His first book *I'd thought you'd be bigger* has been received well and was followed up by his second book entitled *In your face* . This is his third publication to date. Kevin also has also produced a number of his own unique training videos.

July 1999

Copyright Kevin O Hagan 1999©
Published by
New Breed publishing 1999

A CIP catalogue record for this book is available from the British Library

Printed and bound in Great Britain.

ISBN 0 9517567 53

Dedications

Dedication - To all those who seek a peaceful existence but live in the 'real' world.

Special thanks - To Tina 0'Hagan, Paul Flett and Tony Watt for assisting in the photographs.

To lifestyles Fitness Centre for training facilities.

Front cover and book illustrations by Kevin 0'Hagan ©.

Disclaimer
Dedications
Foreword
Introduction
Contents

Chapter 1   To Grapple or not to Grapple?

Chapter 2   A Street fighters strategy on the floor.

Chapter 3   Pinning - Essential control.

Chapter 4   Atemi-Waza.

Chapter 5   A grab-bag of Dirty Tricks.

Chapter 6   Putting out the lights.

Chapter 7   Getting out of a tight spot.

Chapter 8   Destroying grapplings best submissions.

Chapter 9   Cross Armbar- How effective?

Chapter 10   Devastating Anti-rape techniques for ladies.

Chapter 11   One up, one down.

Chapter 12   Fitness and grappling.

Chapter 13   Drills for street grappling.

Chapter 14   A personal insight to advanced ground grappling.

Chapter 15   Will the Real Ju Jutsu stand up, please!

Chapter 16   A final grapple with reality.

Foreword

When I was asked by Kevin to write the foreword to this, Kevin's third book, I was both honoured and surprised. Honoured, because it is a great privilege to write for such an esteemed leader in the field of self-protection. Surprised because, although I have trained and practised various styles for many years, the last four with the Bristol Goshin Jutsu Combat Academy, I am, by no means, an authority on self-protection or the martial arts. I was simply a student of Kevin's who happened also to be criminal defence lawyer. What then could l, a humble lawyer, possibly have to contribute to a book on self-protection by this renowned exponent of the art?

A clue was found in the foreword to Kevin's first book, I Thought you'd be Bigger, which along with his second book, In Your Face, holds pride of place on my bookshelf. In that book, Geoff Thompson, describing Kevin as a 'first rate martial artist' stated that Kevin was one of the few highly graded martial artists who is not afraid to learn from just about anyone that has something of worth to share. This insight into Kevin's personality is precisely what makes him a truly inspirational instructor and self-protection expert. Unlike many mainstream styles whose techniques would be more at home in 17th century Japan, Kevin looks to the streets and people of today's inner cities for inspiration for his own unique and brutally effective style.

Samurai swords do not feature greatly on the streets - bottles, knives and heavy boots do - and Kevin knows it! And unlike many other styles, Kevin doesn't teach techniques as individual acts, but rather he advocates a manner of self-protection that is both fluid and responsive to the environment.

Kevin refers to the techniques of his style as parts of a jigsaw puzzle, each piece (technique) part of a larger whole. If the attacker doesn't respond to one technique, then you move into another.

In this way, each of us was taught to respond to what was physically happening, not to hope that the attacker did this or that and execute the technique regardless. Again, this is the real world - no formal rituals, no time to think. Every technique that Kevin teaches is designed to deal with a real life, in your face, situation.

And with each technique that I learnt and practised, I could see, in my opponent, the faces of the defendants that I saw in court each day (no offence to any of my opponents intended!). And that's how I came to be asked to write this foreword.

You see, as a criminal defence, lawyer, I spent years in police stations, prisons and courts representing the very kind of people that Kevin's style is designed to defend against - real-life murderers, muggers, rapists and robbers. In the evenings, I would attend Kevin's classes and I would delight in telling him, just after he had demonstrated an attack and how to deal with it, 'Yeah, that's the kind of attack that my client used the other night on some poor bastard in the city centre'. I would delight in it because I knew that it meant that what we were doing was real. This wasn't 17th century Japan stuff. This was real-world, real-time self-protection. I'd be thinking that this is what could have happened to me last night if I'd been in the same place, at the same time, as the particular victim that my client had chosen. Kevin was an enthusiastic listener and was always very interested to know the details. Each day that I sat in court, I would hear tales of violence and intimidation perpetrated by thugs and muggers and every time I would hear the details of what they did, I could see in my mind how Kevin's style and training, had it been known to the victim, would have enabled him or her to turn that threat around and put the attacker on the back foot, (or indeed, as with most of Kevin's techniques, on the ground in pain!).

As a lawyer, I had the unique opportunity, unavailable to most students of self-protection, of spending hours talking with my clients, probing them on what they did, and how they chose their victim. And what I learnt from these people is what I can contribute to this book.

I can tell you, without hesitation, that there is not one technique that Kevin teaches that is unrealistic nor one attack that he drills each student, or reader of this book, to protect him or herself against, that has not been used in real life somewhere on the streets of Britain last night or that will not be tried again tomorrow by some thug. What you will read and learn in the following pages happens. People are knocked to the ground. People are kicked senseless on the streets.

I have seen so many victims in court, who, if only they knew how to effectively protect themselves and to grapple once on the ground, could have saved themselves a beating. If you end up on the ground on the street it is a whole lot different to a competition arena. You will need to know tactics and techniques within this text to save yourself a trip to hospital or worse!

Read this book. What you will learn from it is 'reality' of the streets and how to survive.

Matthew Adkins, Solicitor, 1999

B.A.L.L.B.

Preface

This book has been written to clarify where ground-grappling figures in the real world of Self Protection and what constitutes as effective tactics and techniques in this savage and unpredictable arena. The world of Martial Arts has been hit with a deluge of grappling arts within the last two years and everybody at present is riding this tide including grappling and ground fighting into their fighting system.

Everybody unless they have been on planet Mars in recent times will know how effective grappling is as a martial art and they know they have to be training in at least one of it's forms to be an all round martial artist. But it can all get confusing, look at all the styles out there, Brazilian Ju Jutsu, Judo, Sambo, Wrestling, Shoot wrestling etc etc. Which is the best? Which should you be training in? The bottom line is what are you training for? It is easy to get caught up in the whole grappling euphoria and get carried away down a pathway you may not really want to follow or get 'blinkered' in your approach and appraisal of grappling.

This book is going to examine 'street grappling' on the floor and how it will differ to any other ground grappling out there. If you want your grappling to be efficient in the pavement arena you will have to look further than a judo match or no holds barred contest because those things are not 'street grappling'. Hopefully you will know at the end of this book the difference. I hope you will, because the difference could be life or death!

Seriously, I do not self profess myself as some master or 'know it all' expert on ground fighting but I have had a fair amount of experience in all it's fields and have a pretty good idea what works. I have also been lucky enough to train under certain individuals who I believe are Masters of ground grappling but are so humble would never profess so themselves. So armed with this knowledge I will attempt to give you a clear, concise and honest view of how I see 'realistic street grappling'.

Kevin O'Hagan
FEB. 1999

INTRODUCTION

Ground grappling has hit the Martial Arts world as the latest and greatest thing! Just as the 70's had Kung Fu, 80's Kick Boxing and early 90's Ninjutsu, grappling is now the 'in thing'. Everybody is clamouring for the 'bandwagon' that is steadily gaining more and more speed. Is this it?

The ultimate and deadly secret art we have all been waiting for? The answer to every would be Martial Arts experts prayers? If so where has this secret art been hiding and why only now has it surfaced?

The answer is, grappling is as old as man himself. The cavemen first discovered grappling and wrestling as a means of self defence until one of them moved on to picking up a rock and smashing it onto his opponents head and found out how much quicker and effective that was!

Grappling is not new or secret; every civilisation had some form of wrestling or crude grappling. The tombs of the ancient Egyptian Pharaohs had paintings on the walls that depicted forms of grappling. The Greeks had a vicious form of grappling called Panktration that included strikes, gouges, neck breaks and a whole host of other such pleasantries! The Romans had the Gladiatorial Death matches that included grappling and so on and so on.

Wrestling and grappling has been a known practise in many cultures for centuries like India, for example. The ancient Japanese Art of Ju Jutsu had a Form of grappling in armour on the battlefields in feudal times.

In the U.K. itself, the old time bare knuckle boxing contests including it's fair share of grappling with throws like the 'cross buttock' and 'heel trip' used regularly.

Like I mentioned earlier people are looking upon this as a new Martial Art but wrestling particularly in our own U.K. has been there for centuries with different parts of the country specialising in certain styles, hence the wrestling styles of Cumberland, Westmoreland, Cornish etc.

Judo was the first Martial Art to hit our shores particularly at the start of the 1900's although at the time it still carried the name of Ju Jitsu. Judo clubs were teaching all the floor techniques near as damn it that the Brazilian Ju Jutsu systems are teaching now. Yet many Judo clubs have gone out of business from lack of students and revenue because people didn't see it as stylish, yet now hundreds of people are flocking onto mats run by Brazilian Ju Jutsu instructors to practice techniques that Judo men have been practicing for many many years!

In a recent magazine interview Billy Doak a 6th Dan Ju Jutsu instructor of the Goshin Ju Jutsu Association of Wales made a statement along these lines and I tend to agree with him. Also he commented that Ju Jitsu in it's classical form had very little groundwork in it at all and that most techniques finished with one person on the floor and the other standing finishing the encounter with a blow or a lock etc. Again this ties in with the theory of grappling in armour on the battlefields. If you went to the floor rolling around you would have a job to get back up on your feet again.

Don't get me wrong the famous Gracie family are excellent at what they do and have done wonders for grappling in general but it's not their technique that is so superior, it is themselves as top class fighters and athletes.

The same can be said for wrestling, a completely forgotten art by the public. Their only impressions of wrestling was from the televised American WWF fantasies. It was not until wrestlers like Don Frye, Mark Kerr, Randy Colture etc took the no holds barred fighting events by storm that the public began to realise what 'real' wrestling was all about! These guys are monsters on the mat and if they get 'to grips' with you it's all over! Yet as stated wrestling has been around forever.

The recent grappling explosion has lifted the veil over people's eyes and given them a wake up call to the fact that punching and kicking is not enough.

The sleeping giant, which was grappling, has finally awoken and is on the march! Grappling is definitely here to stay this time.

But let's go back a bit and remember what I stated earlier. Yes you must include grappling and floor fighting in your repertoire of skills to be a complete Martial Artist but you must also know what you want out of it and where you want to head with your grappling skills. Sport, competition, no holds barred events are not street grappling. Although all of them take great courage, guts and skill, grappling on the street is a breed apart, now let's find out why!

Chapter One

To Grapple or not to Grapple?

That is the Question!

In a self-protection environment to grapple and go to the floor is not one of the first physical responses in your fighting arsenal. Why? Well the dangers of hitting the ground with your assailant are many fold.

Firstly hitting a cold, hard and un-comprising pavement is a million miles away from hitting the training mats. The pavement has a nasty habit of hurting! Tarmac, gravel, un-even curbs, glass, dog excrement and many other un-welcome problems will greet you. Takedowns and falls executed on the mats will suddenly be very different when your knees, elbows, spine or head come in contact with concrete. You cannot afford to throw yourself about with gay abandonment as in the Dojo.

As I stated in my second book 'In Your Face', Close Quarter fighting', the Brazilians for instance were used to training in a beautiful warm and dry climate, fighting on sandy beaches and lush grassland, so very different to on wet and muddy pavements on a November day in the U.K.!

The thought of launching yourself onto the deck in this countries inclement weather or indeed diving onto the floor in a urine drenched toilet or alcohol wet club floor is not so inviting as a white sandy beach in Rio De Janiro!

Although as mentioned before grappling to the floor and finishing the fight there has proved tremendously effective in the no holds barred fighting arena, so have you to remember there are still rules to protect you.

For example your opponent will not suddenly pull a knife from his boot and start stabbing you in a frenzy. He will not reach out for a disregarded bottle, glass, ashtray etc and club you around the head with it. He will not pull you down tightly and bite your nose off! His mate will not 'wade' in and smash a chair over your head or stab you in the back. Three or four impartial on lookers will not suddenly get the urge to run over and use you both as 'kickbags'. In the street this has a big chance of happening!

Make no mistake if you CHOOSE to take the fight to the floor you have to consider all the above factors and be prepared for them, even if you are you will have a hard job to fend all those things off.

You see this is the un-clouded and un-romantic view of grappling out-side the confines of the controlled arena. It's a whole different 'ball game' and you must get your head out of the clouds to be able to see the pitfalls of grappling as well as it's strengths.

Is grappling going to be the best tactic against more than one opponent?

I don't think so. It would be suicidal to tie yourself up on the ground with one man whilst two or more prepared to tear into you, you would be

kicked senseless.

Is grappling a knife-wielding assailant your best form of defence?

Again not if you can avoid it, you would be foolish to even attempt such an act. So you can see grappling does not carry all the answers, or indeed any one art.

Grappling two attackers? Suicidal!

In a self-protection situation if you couldn't avoid the trouble by escape or verbal persuasion then you would have to launch a pre-emptive strike to win and get away. This has got to be your first choice over any other fighting strategy. This theory is excellently covered in the book, *'Pre- emptive Strikes for Winning Fights'*, by Jamie O'Keefe and *'The Fence'*, by Geoff Thompson. If you failed in this manoeuvre you will probably end up grappling anyway or if your awareness was initially down and you were grabbed you again would most likely be grappling or heading for the floor.

Once you do hit the floor you will be there until one of you finishes it or one of the outside influences I spoke of earlier settles it.

Avoid grappling with weapons

Avoid this situation at all cost!

Multiple opponent attacks are highly dangerous

When to Grapple?
As just stated if you are switched off in a self-protection situation you will be in grappling before you know it. Look how many women are savagely battered or pulled to the ground in rape circumstances. In this instance you will have no choice, it will have already been decided for you.

If you are in an upright grappling situation people have a habit of clinging onto you like a limpet.
Geoff Thompson refers to this as a 'death grip' and even somebody of reasonably light statue can become a strong, determined and desperate adversary un-balancing you and pulling you all over the place.

A friend of mine Mike who is a Doorman told me once of an incident that 'kicked off' with a few guys. He put one of these people away with a 'right hander' and turned just as this young guy steamed into him grabbing at his jacket. Mike is a big guy 6ft 2ins and around 15 stone but he re-called in this instance this lad half his size was freakishly strong and had this so called 'death grip' on him. Mike was pushed back and at that point stepped off the edge of the kerb and fell to the ground with his attacker.
He survived it and won the day but it did shake him and made him much more aware of that particular problem. Again in this instance he was not intending to grapple or go to the floor it just happened.

When the adrenalin is flowing even people who do not look much can become for a short while ultra strong and grip and grapple you like a wild thing, it will not be some controlled wrestling contest it will be a frenzied and violent encounter, also very scary. You may not be able to break their grips, you may well find yourself over-whelmed and even if you take that person down on your terms you will find they will hang on for dear life and probably drag you down with them. Panic, fear and adrenalin makes this happen.

An example outside of the fighting arena is if you have ever tried to stop and rescue somebody from drowning, initially they will thrash about like crazy in panic and almost pull you under with them until they begin to tire and then you can gain control if you know what your are doing. The same can be said of a street-grappling encounter.

To be really good on the floor you have to be highly conditioned with good stamina and muscular endurance. Most un-trained people do not have either of these fitness components in abundance so they will tire quickly. They will for a short time have raw naked strength and an appetite for destruction fuelled on by usually alcohol, drugs or plain jealousy and hatred. For 30 seconds or so they will be your worst nightmare, it will be like grappling with a wildcat or a grizzly bear. You may say 30 seconds isn't too long to whether the storm but what could be done in 30 seconds? How many times could you be head butted and punched? What could be bitten off you in that time? How long does it take to be choked or strangled un-conscious? Or, how many times could you be stabbed?

You see we are not talking mat fighting here! I have hundred's of times on the mat fought bigger and stronger men on the ground and because maybe they didn't have my skill or conditioning or heart beat them when they tired but it may have taken one minute, two minutes or more; a long time to be on the floor in a street situation. Some of the no holds barred contests have gone 30 minutes on the floor, a hell of a long time!

Another occasion you may have to seek the sanctuary of the floor is if in a trade off stand up fight you are taking a battering. If you are getting used as a punch bag and your blows or stand up skills are not getting results you will have to 'clinch' and take it to the floor, hoping that your opponent is not as good as you on the ground. This may be a last ditch tactic out of pure desperation and in that case you can't be blamed for taking it 'down'. It will carry its risks but you will not have much choice in the matter if you were getting battered stood up!

Grappling no matter what people say does rely on body weight and strength to a certain extent. For example think of a big person you may know personally or maybe somebody off the TV. Let's for arguments sake say 'Hunter' from the 'Gladiators' show. He is a big, strong and quick man but as far as I know not any type of trained fighter. Would you even with ground fighting skills want to take him to the floor and wrestle providing you could get him there in the first place! Answer, probably not, unless you also had his size and strength but the average person doesn't so grappling once more would not be your best option (looking for a baseball bat may be a sound option!).

My good pal and fellow self protection instructor Alan Charlton of the Self Protection Association is a mountain of a man and as much as I like ground fighting would not out of choice want to go to the floor and have his 50 stones plus (only kidding Alan) on top of me!

Remember street self protection is very rarely 'match' fighting where two people will agree to have a fight in the car park on equal terms, in that instance if your opponent was say a Taekwondo practitioner and you a Judo man you could well use the tactic of closing him down and taking to the floor but you won't get that luxury, in a street situation you will probably be faced by someone you have never seen before and the time, venue etc will not be of your choosing. The person may possibly be armed or have two or three mates with him so your whole strategy will have to change.
Of course sometimes you may not have a choice and then you will have to make the most of a bad job. The underlying message to this chapter is *learn to fight on the floor but don't go to the floor to fight*.

Remember it's down to choices. If you have to fight on the pavement avoid the floor if you can't, then get it over with quickly

A street attack can happen at anytime!

Chapter Two

A Street fighters Strategy on the floor

In a ground fight outside a controlled arena the average brawler will not be looking to submit you with a cross arm bar, keylock or triangle headlock. He will have no such knowledge of these things. His main priority is to gain a position of dominance so he can punch the living daylights out of you. He will work in a savage burst of energy looking to mount your chest and then start a barrage of punches until either of you are unconscious, he runs out of energy or somebody pulls him off you. He may attempt to kneel on your arms also to trap them and make your face an easier target. If he can pick up a weapon of sorts i.e. bottle, glass, half brick you are in danger of losing your life, most certainly your looks!

If you flail up at him with your arms he will pin them at the wrists and push them down to the ground either side of your head and proceed to head butt your face and/or bite you. The neck, ears, cheeks and nose being the optimum targets.

Clawing at your eyes could be another tactic, as to grabbing your hair or ears and banging your head into the ground. He will then get up and stick a few kicks into you for good measure. Brutal? Yes. Accurate portrayal of how it is? Yes.

What, no strangles, arm locks, leg locks? No.

Street attacker will look to get to a position to punch you out

These are ground fighting tactics based on some pre-historic memories and pure gut reaction for survival. These things have not been learnt in the Dojo or contest arena. To cope with this type of animalistic onslaught you will need more then a handful of submission holds. You will need to re-program your thinking and training to deal with this type of frenzied attack to have any hope of surviving it.

If you fall over, lose your footing or are pushed, knocked or punched to the floor and your assailant is still standing he will not launch himself into a nice scarf hold or a cross body pin, he will opt to stand and kick and stomp bits off you!   Just view any crowd trouble in football matches and you will see what I mean. People have been kicked to death in these circumstances. The floor is the last place on earth you want to go in that situation. So save your leaping, flying and head height kicks for 'playing' around in the Dojo, not for outside. Remember the street fighter is a 'head kicker' but he will wait until you are on all fours or your back before he demonstrates this particular brand of kicking 'Bootwondo' it's called!!

Biting and butting – Two more major tactics

Another concept to take in is also that what you are wearing will effect the issue. A tie for instance can become as deadly garrotte if some-one pulls it tight and takes you down onto your knees with it, it will grip tighter and tighter around the neck and throat and could well end up throttling you. Geoff Thompson describes an account of this happening in one of his 'Ground Fighting' series of books.

Anything will go! Have you got the bottle!

A jacket, jumper can be pulled over your head to impair your vision and breathing and can be very awkward to escape from. Also if you are into wearing your hair long gentlemen you can give your attacker one hell of a 'handle' to gain painful leverage and control of your head. Any trendy facial piercing like ears, nose, eyebrows etc can suddenly become extremely painful trinkets when ripped from your skin! NASTY!

Clip on ties get you over the problems of throttling, a lot of door personnel wear these, not sure about a 'Rodney Trotter' clip on pony tail though, best to get a hair cut!

If you find yourself in an upright grapple you could well find you may get caught in a side head lock and normally you will be taken down with the headlock still on, again don't expect a submission hold to follow, expect punches and gouges to your trapped head. How to escape the standing headlocks are adequately described in my book, 'In your Face' - Close quarter fighting.

So those are the tactics to mainly anticipate in street grappling when it hits the deck. You must start to train against these type of attacks, this is a far cry from any competition grappling, this is the 'real deal'.

As brilliant grapplers the Gracies are, when they first constructed the rules for the ULTIMATE FIGHTING CHAMPIONSHIPS, biting and eye gouging were not allowed. Obviously this was to keep the format as humane as possible and make it acceptable for TV networks but also they were astute enough to know these things can ruin a grapplers day!

In training be careful and train sensibly, there is no need to 'brain' each other senseless. But steadily increase the pressure as you get used to this type of training.

Get one man to wear a pair of fingerless boxing gloves and he can punch away at you. Touch biting to a nip and touch fingers to eyes can let you know he got there and then you grapple back and see how difficult it becomes to put on a standard submission hold, you will be hit from every angle and remember what I said earlier about the 30 second rule?
Time just 30 seconds and see what the other guy can get through with. When you do this first time it is a bit eye opener and a humbling experience. Give it a go.

Finally a good example of the un-predictable beating a good fighter on the floor was demonstrated clearly in the videotape 'The World Combat Championships'.

Renzo Gracie one of the Gracie clan fought a very experienced Judo man from the Netherlands, I'm afraid I don't recall his name. Anyway when the fight went to the floor it was all pretty even. Gracie finally got to the 'mounted' position and then head butted the Judoka in the face.

Now obviously this man knew it was a limited rules contest and the headbutt was legal but he couldn't have trained for it or been mentally prepared, because in pain he turned giving Gracie his back and a chokehold to win the bout. As I mentioned this guy was a top class Judoka but a tactic that he wasn't used to dealing with in his floor work beat him. We should all learn a valuable lesson form this!

On the pavement arena anything goes!

What you don't know or expect – will beat you!

Chapter Three

Pinning - Essential Control

Now that we have examined all the negatives about being on the floor what positives can we draw out of the situation?

One thing that the untrained man will lack on the ground along with endurance is balance. If he hasn't practised any skilled grappling his balance will be poor. In my experience as his stamina begins to sap his balance gets worse and he can be quite easy to pin or turn.

If you have good knowledge of balance and spreading your weight you have the most essential tool in ground fighting.

People tend to look at the various submissions, like leg locks, armbars and strangles and believe they are the key to ground grappling, they are not, they are the finishing product of good pinning skills. Without being able to control somebody on the floor with a pin you will have little or no chance of finishing them.

When the fight hits the floor your untrained opponent will be like a wild, frenzied beast. If he is underneath you he will be bucking and thrashing around like a lunatic. You have got to learn to evenly distribute your weight and weather the storm. Pretty soon the unconditioned individual will run out of steam and his energy will disperse like air from a deflating balloon. Then you can go for your finish.

To try and get an accurate picture of the need to control. Picture a surfer, he is keen to ride the big waves and become an expert at doing so, but first he must be able to balance in the water comfortably on his surfboard before he has any hope of taming the waves. Imagine a rodeo rider wanting to tame that wild steer he's riding, firstly he's got to learn to hold on long enough on it's back and not fall off. Finally think about how you would get up onto a plastic lilo in a swimming pool, this involves distributing your weight evenly otherwise you just fall off again or the lilo flips up and flies away from you!

Any of the above illustrations can be applied to control and pinning on the ground.

All floor systems put great emphasis on floor control, be it Judo, wrestling or Ju Jutsu, without it's like clinging onto a flower stem in a gale force wind.

The Pins

I am going to briefly describe the basic pins and I will just use lay-mans terms and no Japanese terminology, that some of you may be familiar with. First we will look at the 'SCARF HOLD'. This is my favourite holding position and one of the strongest ground positions to find yourself in.
Study the photograph of the position and the way the body is positioned the distribution is vital for the hold to work.

Sit around the right side of your opponents body resting your weight onto the side of his chest and ribs. This is like standing on a bathroom scales and then reaching down and pulling up with your hands on the bottom of the scales. It's increasing the reading of your weight considerably. This is the feeling your opponent will have on his body. Now put your right arm around his neck. Place it on the floor, or grasp your trouser leg or grab behind your opponents collar. You can increase pressure on his ribs by pulling his right elbow close to your left side with your left hand, rolling your left shoulder backwards. Split your legs like a hurlers going over a hurdle. Your right foot out in front, your left splayed back. Your legs balance your weight evenly and your feet act as brakes. If your opponent attempts to pull you back or forward your feet will dig in accordingly and stop your balance from being disturbed. When you have secured this position you are in a strong location to finish the fight.

Next up, the CROSS BODY PIN. You in this instance are lying horizontally across your opponents body. Your chest is pressing directly into his chest.

Your knees are drawn up, one under his armpit and one by his hip. Your arms are pulled in tight, elbows controlling his far hip and side of neck.

Your pelvis is pushed down into the ground, this drops your centre of gravity and distributes your weight evenly: Again study the photograph.

During the ensuing struggle you may find you have to tripod out one or both legs and get up onto the balls of your toes to shift your weight, also you may have to change your hand positions somewhat. As long as one monitors the head and one a hip you will still have control. Do bear in mind all the time your opponent is not only to be lying there like a 'dead body so you will have to monitor his movements and adjust accordingly..

This can only be done from plenty of 'live' practise in training.

We move on to the 'MOUNT POSITION'. In the art of Brazilian Ju Jutsu this is known as the superior position to achieve. It can be a strong position to strike from but it does require practise to maintain your balance and position. Refer to photos. There are basically two positions. A high mount where you will sit up high, knees either side of opponents chest and tight up into his armpits, you are now in the best position to strike from.

Initially when you move to the mount you may be in the low mount position.

This time you are further down the body your butt and hips controlling his hips, your feet tight to his legs or entangling them. This low position prevents him from 'bucking' up his hips and throwing you off. Your hands can 'post' wide on the ground either side of his head or you can lie your upper body down on him. To maintain this position think of the 'table theory' your body is a table with four legs. Your two hands and two knees, in this instance.

If you allow one or more 'legs' to be removed the table will topple, in this case you! Again practise is the key to maintaining the mount, there is no other way to get that feel for it.

The fourth position is the 'top body pin'.

On this occasion you are above opponent kneeling at the top end of his head. Lean over and let your chest smother his face. Grip over his arms and onto his trouser belt, pockets or link your hands together under his lower back. Now drop your pelvis to the floor and either have both knees up either side of his ears, or one or both legs again stretched back, up on the toes. This is another very strong pinning position but you will have to relinquish it to get a good finish.

Next the 'reverse scarf hold'.
This time you are sitting facing opponents feet. Wrap his right arm around your waist holding it tightly against your body with your right hand. Now put the left side of your body over your opponents upper chest and neck. Place your left arm underneath his left arm above the elbow. Grab his belt, trousers with your left hand.
Splay your legs again in hurdle position and lean your upper back and shoulder into his face. It is a surprisingly strong position but once more not a great finishing position.

These are the 5 basic top positions for control, with training you should be able to use transition and move around the body in and out of these positions keeping your weight based low and over your opponent. You want to be familiar with all these pins but you will probably get to favour one or two the best. To learn how to fully drill these pins, I recommend reading 'The Pins' from Geoff Thompson's ground grappling series of books.

For the scope of this book a working knowledge will be sufficient for the street. There are two more positions on the floor that need to be examined. Firstly the 'Guard'.

This position is highly favoured by the Brazilian fighters and they use it to great effect. You will be on your back for this position with your legs wrapped around your opponents waist. You can wrap around tightly and pull opponent down towards you to control him; this is called the 'closed guard', which is more defensive in nature.

You can open up your legs and put your feet on your opponents hips to monitor your opponents movements. This is the 'open guard' and is more attacking in nature. The guard essentially stops your opponent climbing onto the mounted position on your chest and is a terrific hold to know when on your back.

If you train it enough it will be very difficult for the average person to get past.

The 'Knee on position'

This is a transitional position.

You can get to it from the 'Cross body pin'.

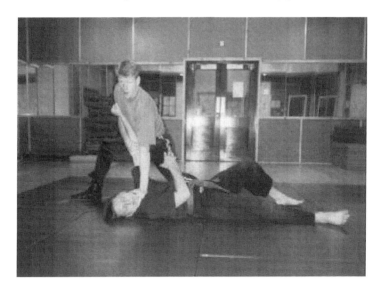

Just 'pop up' and put your knee onto your opponents chest or mid-section. This restricts the chest from expanding and drawing in air, it is very uncomfortable for the person on the receiving end. From this position you can effectively strike and control. You could also change the knee and kneel onto opponents head or neck which is incredibly painful.

Again the Brazilian fighters used this position a lot and there are some pretty fancy mobility drills you can work for swapping the 'knee on' position but we will just stick with the basic move outlined above.

Remember as previously mentioned you will have to practise the pins to get a good feel for them and to be confident in holding them on a fighting opponent. When you do achieve a degree of skill in doing it you will feel a lot more happier about control on the floor. 'Control and pinning is the key to winning'!

'PIN TO WIN'

Chapter Four

'Atemi-Waza'

'Vital Strikes on the Floor'

To finish the fight quickly on the floor you must be able to strike from every given position with power and accuracy. Knowledge of Atemi-waza (vital points striking), is crucial to coming out on top. Striking has got to be your main artillery when street grappling, not submission holds. Why?
Because you can't be looking to get your attacker to 'tap out', because he will not have heard of such a thing, he has no concept of it! Tapping out is a signal of submission in the competitive arena to prevent serious injury; on the street you are looking possibly at a life and death situation. If you succeed in getting an arm bar on your attacker he may well yell 'stop, stop your breaking my f-----g arm, let go, I give up'. But how do you know, you could release him and he will jump up and pull a knife on you and now you have lost control of the situation. I can speak from experience, some people are very devious and will plead compliance one second and be battering you the next! It's like grabbing the collar of a savage dog and controlling it, if it calms down would you choose then to release it or not?
How would you know it's not going to bite you as soon as you do, the same can apply to a human.

Strikes will settle the issue and get you back to your feet quickly which remember is your MAIN PRIORITY. The longer you are down there on the ground the more vulnerable you become.
Let's examine the strikes available to you from the previously described pinning positions.

THE MOUNT

This is a superior position for striking. Sit up, high knees, right up under opponents armpits and make your knees grip and hug tightly to his ribs. From here with your weight based you can punch two-handed down onto your opponents face. Alternatively you may opt to grip his windpipe with one hand for balance and punch with your strongest hand. If you don't want to punch use the heel of your hand, it's very powerful and destructive. Even if your assailant covers his face your heel hand can batter away without fear of injury to yourself.

Your elbows can be used like battering rams to strike horizontally into the face. Base one hand on the floor and strike with the other or alternate.

If opponent grips you around the waist elbow downwards onto the vulnerable top of the head and base of the skull. The head butt can be used by firstly pinning down the arms of your aggressor onto the floor. Do this at the junction of his elbow joints and biceps, this is a powerful pin and controls his shoulders and upper arms, much better than grabbing the wrists to pin.

Now you can batter your head down to great effect! If you are pulled down close you can begin to bite at any exposed target and also thumb gouge the eyes if necessary. When released you can grab the hair or ears of the assailant and bang his head on the ground. If assailant begins to turn onto his side, pin his jaw down with the heel of your hand and strike to exposed jaw, ear or temple.

If he turns to his belly, strike to neck/spine area, hook punch the temples. If he covers up back of head with his hands, grip hold of a finger (especially the little one) and yank it back to break, again exposing the head. There are other things we can do from this position but we will look at them later under another heading.

Once your attacker is knocked out or incapacitated get to your feet quickly, using your pushing body weight on your hands to jump up to a knee on the chest position before getting off his body. This is a safety method of getting up whilst still under control, which is an important factor.

ELBOW STRIKING FROM THE MOUNT

SCARFHOLD
This strong holding position offers you a few choice strikes when available.
Firstly you need to 'tie off' your opponents near side arm, so he cannot cover his face. You do this with your legs (refer to photos), now you can punch or palm heel into the face or neck. Head butting can be done from here as can eye gouging and clawing techniques. If you lose control of his head, lean your weight back on him and back elbow strike to the head.
This is about the most practical Atemi from this hold.

THUMB TO THE EYE–A FINISHER FROM A SCARFHOLD

CROSS BODY

From here you can make good use of knee strikes into the ribs or the head and neck, depending which knee you strike with. Get good height on the knee and then drive it down in to the exposed targets. This requires some practise to get right, best to try it on a punch bag lying on the floor.

Back elbows can be used to ribs and head in the opposite direction on the other side of his body. If you cradle up his neck and head you can drive home a series of head butts. Pinning his jaw to the floor gives you an opening for a downward elbow strike or grind into the temple. Reaching down and seizing the testicles will get his attention as will finger digging into the femoral artery/nerve in the groin area. Elbowing the outer side of the thighs can have a 'dead leg' effect. Remember you can bite to any exposed area particularly if you are being held tightly. Also when you get a chance jump up to the 'Knee on position' and strike down onto your opponent and then regain your upright posture.

ELBOW TO THE TEMPLE, FROM CROSS BODY PIN!

TOP BODY PIN

This pin offers little opportunity of a great finishing strike but you still can do some damage with a little imagination.

You can knee strike the top of his head and get in a short knee drop to the forehead if you're quick enough. Also again if you're fast you may be able to 'pop up' and launch a downwards head butt to the face. Eye gouging and throat clawing can also be neutralised.

REVERSE SCARFHOLD

Even more limited strike options than the previous pin. As stated before it is more of a half way household before moving onto a stronger position. Back elbows to the face are possible as to is reaching down and grabbing the testicles, that's about it really.

THE GUARD

In the closed guard you can pull attacker down onto head-butts and bites.

Short hooks to the temples and heel kicks into the kidney area. Grabbing hair, ears or head and chin you can twist opponent off you. Thumb gouging the eyes is also available.

If opponent is more upright, punching and palm heeling the face becomes an option. You can also go to open guard, control his hips and then kick with the soles of your feet into his face/chest and then regain your feet.

Which remember is your priority.

Also another position for attack is when your opponent is on all fours.

If you are not being held in anyway jump to your feet and kick directly into his face or if to the side his ribs. Also stomping down onto his hands from the front or his 'Achilles heel' from the rear are great tactics.

If being held at opponents head end, then knee strike to his head and elbow down onto the spine until you get a release, then back to your feet and continue as previously mentioned.

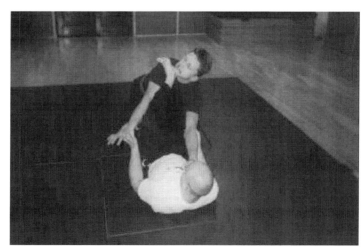

OPEN GUARD, KICK TO FACE

CLOSE GUARD, GOUGE FOR A RELEASE

KNEE STRIKING THE SKULL

Striking is always going to be the quickest and best method for street grappling but it has to be practised over and over to make it work and you will have to be in some kind of shape because it can take a lot out of you.

We will look later at how to drill these strikes properly. You must be able to target the areas you need to strike and be able to get powerful impact into your blows. You must also keep up a continual barrage and be able to change from one ground position to another with ease to make yourself as elusive a target as possible.

Striking is your first and foremost tactic to finish a ground fight outside, don't forget this and you can survive.

Chapter Five

'A grab - bag of Dirty Tricks'

The techniques contained in the following pages are a random selection of brutal survival methods culled from Atemi Jutsu/Kempo, C.Q.B. Ju Jutsu and my own methods of combat for ground fighting. They are not pretty and in some cases you may think extreme, but remember we are talking about:
fighting for our very lives on the pavement arena! No referees, whilstles, bells or rules, no time duration, trophies or medals. This is the 'real deal', you must know the following techniques to have an 'edge' when needed and be able to execute them without conscience.

Some of the techniques are finishers; others will act as painful manipulators. I have not used any text to explain their applications; I will let the photos do the talking! Treat them with respect and use them as your surprise equalisers when the chips are down.

THE TOP TEN NASTIES
(Accompanying music is optional)

Clawing and Gouging

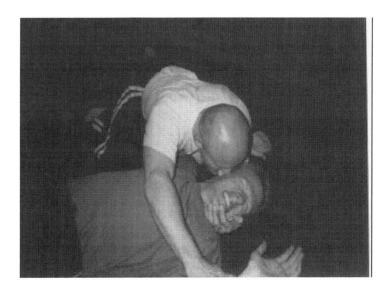

Biting

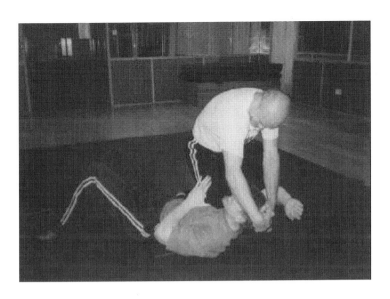

Neck Cranking

Neck Wrenching

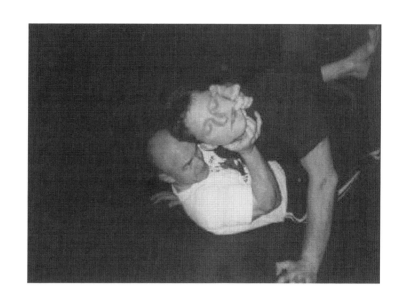

Fish Hooking Mouth

Nose/ Face Barring

Hair Pulling / Eye Clawing

Nostril Ripping

Choking/ Pressure Point Gouging

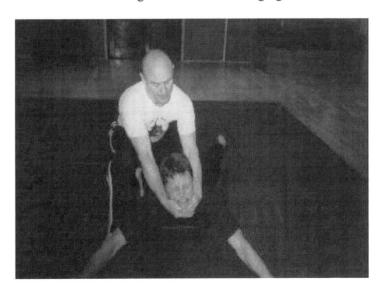

Neck And Spinal Stretching

Grinding Elbow in Eye Socket/ Squeezing Testicles

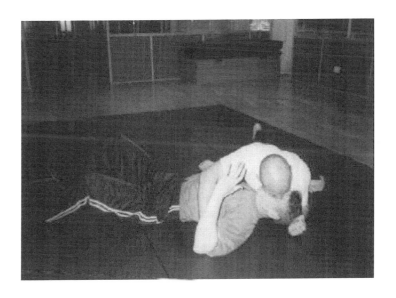

"Brucie Bonus" Grinding Chin into Eye Sockets!

Chapter Six

'Putting the Lights Out

Chokes and Strangles

Chokes and strangles are right up there with striking as the next effective finisher to a ground grapple. A properly applied hold can take your opponents consciousness away very quickly and win the day for you. A choke or strangle executed even by a child can have an immediate effect on a large adult.

I am going to deal with straightforward and relatively easy chokes and strangles to execute. In the realms of Judo, Ju Jutsu and other such arts there are a myriad of such moves but we will just deal with the basic necessities for no holds barred combat.

In my first book, 'I thought you'd be bigger', I explained in some detail the working anatomy of the neck, so I won't go over old ground again,

I suggest you refer to the above book for that information.

Basically a choke restricts air through the windpipe and a strangle drastically slows the blood flow to the brain from the carotid arteries.

The carotid strangle or 'sleeper hold' is a more humane method to execute on somebody as consciousness usually returns quickly. A choke sometimes carries the danger of the windpipe collapsing and death may occur.

Once more any of these holds should be treated with respect and used in the dangerous situations we are discussing in this book. They should not be played with and you should seek supervision of a qualified instructor to practise them correctly.

Below are two illustrations to show the difference between a choke and a strangle.

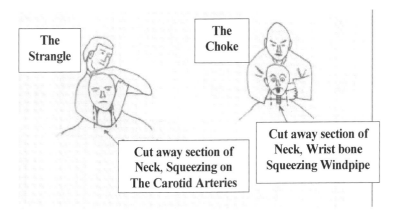

The Strangle

The Choke

Cut away section of Neck, Squeezing on The Carotid Arteries

Cut away section of Neck, Wrist bone Squeezing Windpipe

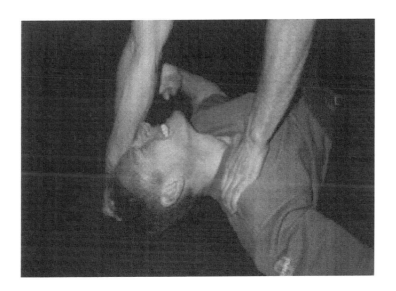

Thumb Gouge to Jugular Notch!

STRANGLES/CHOKES from the Mount

This position offers you the greatest opportunity to initiate a strangle or choke. You can apply these either by using a collar or lapel of a jacket or you can use bare handed methods referred to as 'naked' chokes or strangles (Don't be alarmed you can keep your clothes on!)

You can execute the holds on a T-shirt but the fabric will stretch and possibly rip so sometimes it may not be worth the risk. If you do decide to work on a T-shirt take up as much slack as possible in your hands, the T shirt will not stretch out too far and be under too much strain.

A sturdy leather jacket or suit jacket will be more tolerant to the gripping and pulling. Remember you must practise wearing this type of clothing, as it is vital to be familiar where and how to grip real street clothing and not just a Gi top (traditional Martial Arts jacket).

The bare handed methods are more readily available and easier to execute.

Also most people's necks are weak and vulnerable to the strangle or choke.

People within grappling build up certain conditioning to their necks and get used to being put in chokeholds etc, psychologically they are also conditioned to receive these holds and an experienced grappler will not panic like a novice.

If you constrict the average persons breathing they will panic like crazy because they think they are going to die! Their heart rate will increase rapidly as well their breathing and blood pressure will rocket up. All these things will only aid the chokehold coming on more quickly. This is why these holds are so effective but also so dangerous!

Study the photos and accompanying text to see these practical strangles and chokes in action. Remember I have chosen the one's most suited to street grappling.

1. VICE CHOKE

Control back of neck with one forearm, slip other forearm across windpipe and then grab your own arms or sleeves to form a vice. Now lean your weight in onto the windpipe for the choke.

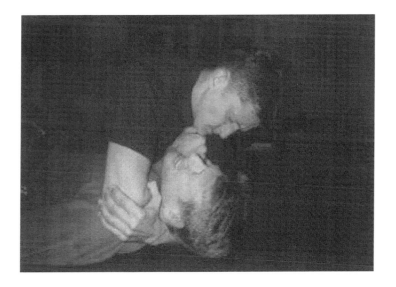

2. JAPANESE HEADLOCK AND STRANGLE

The Brazilians refer to this hold as the 'lion kill'. As most wild beasts, mount their preys back and attack their necks. In this instance your attackers has turned to his belly to avoid your blows. You continue striking back of his head until he looks up exposing his neck. Now wrap an arm right around the neck, constricting the carotid arteries. Join hand to other bicep, other hand pushes down on head, squeeze tight to apply strangle.

i.e. You can also raise his head by gouging a knuckle into the mastoid cavity behind the ear lobe or hooking up the eyes or nostrils or executing the face bar. Also remember if we are street grappling pushing the attackers face down into a puddle, mud, urine, beer etc will have him coming up gasping for air, then you can clamp on the strangle.

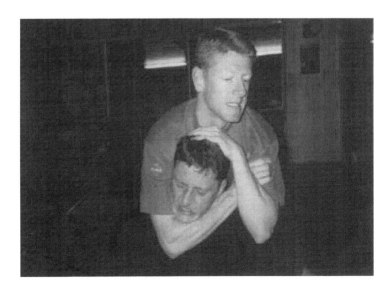

3. REAR BODY SCISSORS WITH STRANGLE

If in the previous technique your opponent gets to his knees, you can stick your heels into his hips (this is called digging your spurs in),and either bear the weight of your pelvis down on his back and flatten him again or cling on and roll onto your back, holding him in the scissor guard and carrying on with the strangle.

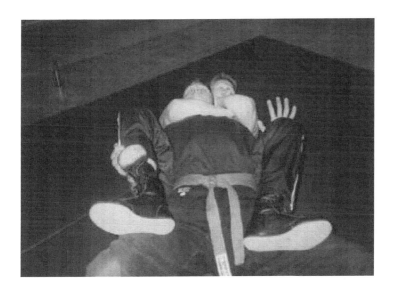

4. WRAP AROUND CHOKE

In this instant for example grab his right lapel with your right hand and pull it across to his left. Now let your left hand wrap around the back of his neck and then take hold of his right lapel from your right hand. Come up onto one knee and pull back strongly on his lapel to form shearing pressure across his throat. This is an excellent choke and one of my personal favourites.
I have executed many times to win the day in grappling situations!

In one such situation against a strong opponent I managed to feed his T-shirt collar across with my teeth so I could link up the final grip. This is pure survival and innovation under pressure!

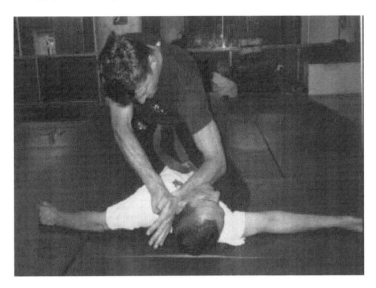

5. A straight clawing grip to the windpipe can work well, as each lapel and driving your thumbs or knuckles into each side pipe causing a nasty 'gagging' type of choke. See photos.

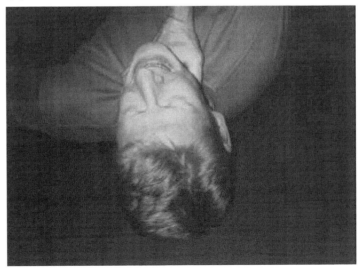

Finishing from the Scarfhold

1. KNUCKLE CHOKE

For the scarf hold the best and most immediate finish is the knuckle choke.
You firstly have to entrap and 'tie off' opponents near side arm, then drive your fore knuckles hard into the side of the windpipe to get an instant effect.

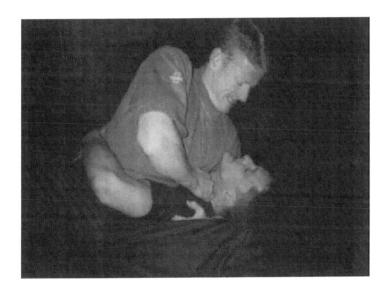

2. ARM TRAP STRANGLE

If you don't entrap opponents arm he may well push his hand up under your chin or claw for your eyes. You let your head yield back and then knock his arm across his body at the elbow. Immediately drive your shoulder and head deep down under his shoulder, as you link up your arms. Tripod up onto your knee and go to a cross body position, sinking down on hips and you tightly execute this strangle, which also becomes a neck lock. Done right it's like having your head stuck in a vice!

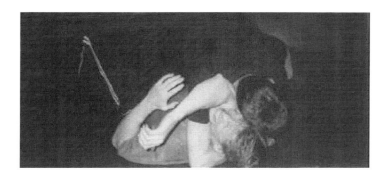

Finishing from the Cross Body

1. SCOOP CHOKE

Cradle your opponents neck up with one arm and then bring your other up his chest palm up and link up your hands. Push in vigorously on his neck to execute a very quick and potent choke on the windpipe.

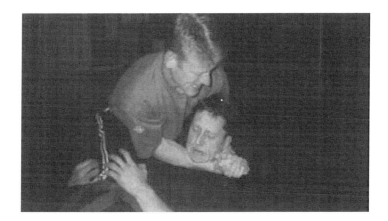

2. FOREARM CHOKE

Grip his far lapel or shoulder with your nearest hand and drop your forearm against his throat. Keep your elbow down low and lean your weight onto his throat to perform this simple but effective choke.

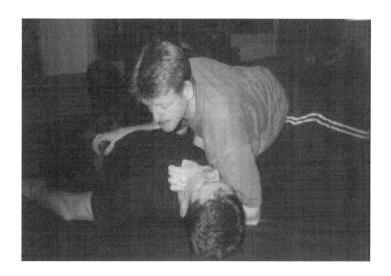

Finishes from under the guard

1. ARM TRAP STRANGLE

As described previously, look at change in my hand position.

2. FIG 8 CHOKE

Grab for example opponents right lapel up high with your right hand. Get your right forearm under his chin. Now circle the back of his neck with your left arm and join your left hand into the crook of your right elbow.

Push up with your right hand into his throat and down with your right elbow to tighten the figure 8 choke.

3. LOOP OVER STRANGLE

For this one, grab opponents right lapel halfway down with your right hand, fingers inside. Grab high,: up on back of his collar on the same side with your left hand, thumb inside. Now jerk his head forward and loop your left arm over to the left side of his neck. You now have a cross strangle on, pull your elbows down in a 'scissoring' motion to clamp into the carotid arteries. As you pull his face down, clamping your teeth onto his nose will give him something extra to worry about!

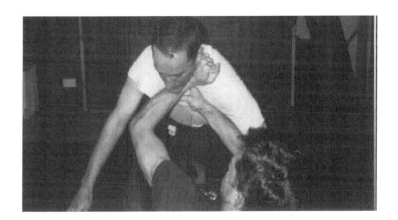

4. WRAP AROUND CHOKE

As described previously will work also from this position

.

The top pin or reverse scarf holds don't really carry any great chokes or strangles of note for practical use on the streets, so we won't bother with them. Getting yourself into one of the previously mentioned positions is a better and quicker option. Another position is again the 'all fours position' you are kneeling at the head end of your attacker. Immediately encircle his head/neck with your right arm and join up with your left hand. Get the blade of your right forearm against the windpipe and then lever up in a front guillotine choke and neck lock.

If attacker turns his head to the side it becomes more of a neck lock. You can finish on your knees, sprawl back onto your belly or jump into the guard.

As mentioned earlier there are dozens of strangles and chokes you can execute with your arms and legs. But most are not really practical for the live environment of the street. Best to stick with the tried and tested ones outlined in this chapter. Remember we are not fighting an expert ground fighter, you are concerned with dealing with the average thug on the street.

Other methods of practical choking, strangling and smothering.

1. Tie choking
2. Smothering with jacket/jumper
3. Garrotting with cord.
4. Obscuring and smothering with hat.
5. Strangled with own scarf.
6. Suffocated with a plastic bag.
7. Ducking in water.
8. Smothered by blankets/pillow.

You may have to use these methods or you could fall foul to them yourself, so beware that there are many methods of losing your breath!

If in Doubt, Choke Him Out

Strangling with a Tie

Garrotting with a Cord

Smothering

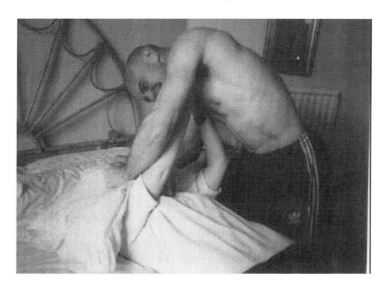

Suffocating (Plastic Bag)

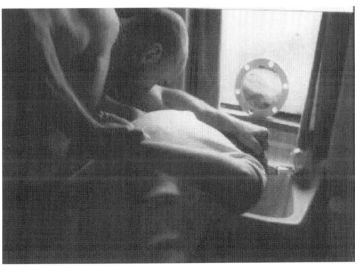

Drowning

Chapter Seven

Getting out of a Tight Spot

In the opening chapter we looked at what the average street attacker will attempt to do to you on the floor. Remember his main objective were to get in a position to pummel you with strikes. Sometimes he will unknowingly get into pins or holds similar to what we have previously described. You will have to know what to do to escape these disadvantageous positions and get back in control. We will examine how to counter some holds on the floor with simple but practical techniques.

Countering a scarf hold

Even an untrained opponent will end up getting on a crude version of a scarf hold if you let him. If this happens do not get caught flat on your back. Turn in towards opponent onto your nearside hip. This will enable you to have some space and movement. Prevent your nearest arm from being controlled by tucking in your elbow. Now let your furthest hand come up and over to rake into your attackers eyes or nostrils to pull his head back and un-balance him. You could also use the fishhook to the mouth. Making sure you stretch and pull on the cheek before inserting fingers inside the mouth to avoid a bite!

You could use the wrap around collar strangle described elsewhere in the book or grab the hair or tie if available for the same effect. Pull opponent back viciously and 'scoot' your hip away getting up onto your knees into a more commanding position.

Another option would be to use your nearest hand and fire a rapid finger spear into opponents eyes or throat or grip the windpipe and squeeze to gain control.

Countering the Mount

Remember this is the last place you want to find yourself in a fight, under the mount. You must except to take some punishment here, your job is to minimise the amount.

Immediately reach up and pull attacker down to you and bite into an ear, cheek, etc, twist the chin and head sharply to roll him off of your body.
Another method is to pull him down and thumb gouge the eye or jugular notch (indentation at base of windpipe). Double slapping the ears and grabbing them and twisting the head is effective, as to is grabbing the testicles to get him to shift position.

If attacker jams a forearm across your throat, knock his arm across the body and apply the arm strangle discussed previously.
If he is attempting a double handed throttle, reach and grab for the little finger and yank it back to break it, hold on and twist it for control.

You will also have to practise covering up and blocking punches before you get your moves on. Practise steadily with a 'gloved up' partner to get a feel of what to do.

Countering a cross body

If your attacker is lying across you attempting a pin or snatching a breather, then bite into the flesh around his ribs, this will shift his weight and give you a chance to escape or make a 'hole' for you to get your knee/shin in against his body and then work yourself into the more favoured guard position.

Elbowing the ribs and kidneys is worth trying, also is reaching between his legs and squeezing the testicles.

Under guard

From here you can work any of the atemi strikes and chokes/strangles that we have previously described. Remember being able to get up is a priority unless for some reason you have to stay down. Maybe this opponent is a good upright fist fighter or boxer or a good kick boxer so you want him down in an environment he is not used to and finish there. If this is your tactic, fine, but still be careful.

Top Pin

If your opponent is trying to choke or throttle you from kneeling above your head, then reach up and grab his ears and pull his head forward into a barrage of knee strikes to the crown. Twist him over sharply by the ears onto his back and then slam a couple of downward elbows into his face to finish.

Under an 'all fours position'.

Your attacker has you around the body or similar on an all fours (refer to photo). You immediately grab and hug one of his arms and spin quickly over onto your back so you end up on top of him. Straight away go to work on your striking to escape and get up.

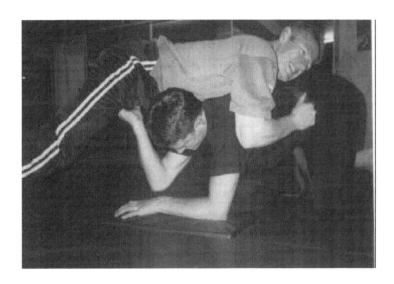

On the floor you can end up in many weird and wonderful positions, these are the most common even against a relatively un skilled person. As stated there are dozens of counters and escapes, but for the purpose of this book and street grappling you must go for the direct, simple and brutal approach to survive, we are not having: a wrestling match here we are fighting for our lives.

Q: Where does a 400lb Gorilla sit?
Ans: Anywhere it bloody well likes!

Chapter Eight

'Destroying grapplings best submissions'

This was a slightly difficult chapter to write, as I have for many years trained on perfecting and drilling a variety of submission holds and have had good success with them in the competitive arena. But the best submission holds in the competitive field, no matter how limited rules will not always be the great finishers on the street. Why? Because we have to look at that element of the un-expected and the fact you are fighting the most unpredictable of opponents, the 'street fighter'! They do not think or function like a trained fighter and in this case, grappler. Their skill is based on the primitive survival function, any thing goes to win. If you are not prepared for this or indeed conditioned and train yourself psychologically to also be this way inclined you will fall foul of their methods.

When two skilled grapplers meet they sub-consciously fight within certain boundaries, even in no holds barred events they are not looking to seriously maim or kill their opponent. In a 'live fight' there is a big possibility of this happening and people reacting out of fear, pain and panic can do some pretty nasty and un-expected things. Be warned, a good skilled fighter can be beaten by these things.

Let's examine a choice few of the most common submission holds and how they can be defeated in a totally no rules what so ever arena! Then I will show a possible alternative to counter what has been done.

BREAKING THE GUARD

I have seen people in this position for a long long time and have struggled desperately to escape it. Firstly you need to kneel up in the guard and prevent your head being controlled.

Remember in this environment the opponent will bite you or ram a thumb into your eye socket!

In the controlled arena if you ground grapple without a jacket, you may be able to stay head down for ages, as your sweaty head and body makes it difficult for a finish. But in the street it is a different matter.

If you are wearing a jacket and you are against an experienced grappler, he will make you pay the price for keeping your head down.

A few years back I grappled with a good judo man, named Ian, who trains in Newport, he is a real gentleman but a monster of a man! He's got to be 6ft 4ins and 17st plus. It's like wrestling a grizzly bear, his arms and legs are like tree trunks!

Anyway we were jacket wrestling and I made the mistake of keeping my head low whilst in his guard and he grabbed my lapel and looped over a incredibly tight cross collar strangle. I can take a bit of stick and it's got to be something special to make me 'tap out' and this hold was just that! It snapped on my carotid arteries like a vice and the black spots were appearing before my eyes, I just had time to tap out to avoid a 'deep sleep'. I learned by lesson well and keep my head up and back straight after that!

So make sure you do this, now jump up onto your feet. If your opponent keeps the guard on you will have stretched up his pelvis and hips off the floor. Now you can execute your finisher, a good, hard punch in the b-----k's! Simple, yes. Effective, definitely, it works every time, you are now out of the guard!

So you don't get caught on the receiving end of such a technique, when lifted, turn onto a hip and bring your shin/knee across their body, this protects your groin and still gives you a degree of protection. You will have to drill it to get the feel.

COUNTERING A TRIANGLE HEADLOCK

Study the photograph of this technique, it is a advanced finisher and takes much practise to get right. When you have it, the legs can put vice like pressure on the neck, it's like sticking your head in a bear trap. To counter it as the opponents leg snakes around the neck, turn in and bite into the tender flesh at the top of his thigh on the inner side. This is excruciatingly painful and will most certainly prevent him from closing the triangle off; your teeth are also hovering fairly close to the genitals (all's fair in love and war!). If you get your triangle headlock on, a better option is shown in the next photograph. After the head is trapped go for a double thumb gouge to the eyes or relentlessly punch the face, a quicker controller and finisher.

CROSS ARMBAR COUNTER

This is a big submission finisher and once the elbow is straightened out its game, set and match! So as you find yourself caught in position for the appending arm bar, turn in on your hip and pull your elbow in and down, immediately grab the ankle of the leg across your face and bite hard into the calf muscle, this will shift opponents position and give you a chance to escape.

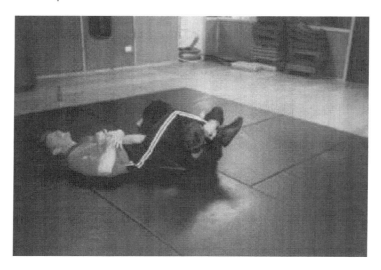

If you apply the arm bar look at the second photograph and notice my leg position still controlling but not exposed to a bite.

Sometimes an experienced opponent will prevent the straightening of the arm by going to the 'catch' position (Photo 3). There are many fancy ways of breaking this hold, some effective, some not so. The best methods for reality are link his arm with one of yours and hammer fist his nose with your other or his solar plexus, depending on which arm you favour, then kick hard into his bicep with your heel to get control for your finish.

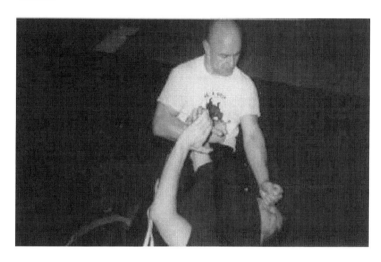

Fig. 4 ELBOW LOCK

Another popular submission and a good one. But check out photo one to see an unexpected move by your opponent!!! If you were exactly controlling a knife arm then this is a strong hold. You can rub and grind the back of his knife hand along the concrete and snap on the elbow lock to gain a knife release. Sinking your teeth into the bicep is a 'Brucie Bonus !'

Note: Knife in free hand Stabbing Body!

REAR CHOKE OR STRANGLE

To counter this you need to shrug up your shoulders and lower your chin making it difficult to get at your windpipe. Then pull down on attackers arm and bite into his forearm and then grab his little finger and snap it.
Your rear head butt can then smash back into his face and you can get a release.

For you to finish with a good strangle, you must pull up on the head to expose that neck. Methods discussed before like the nostril rip, eye claw or face bar should do the trick!

As stated these are just a selection of the most popular submissions, of course there are many, many more but you can see they are all not foolproof all the time, nothing is a 100% guaranteed. Hopefully this chapter will make you more aware of this fact.

'What you don't know will hurt you'

'Expect the unexpected'

OOHHH !
I didn't
Expect that !

Chapter Nine

Cross Arm bar - How Effective?

Jujigatame or cross arm bar has got to be the most practised and used of all joint lock submissions. Every video on grappling shows it, every magazine includes it in its grappling articles. Just how effective is it for the street? Firstly, there is no doubt when this arm bar is put on it is extremely effective, without any argument.   When you see a world-class grappler like Judo champion Neil Adams working it, he does it with an ease that is unbelievable to behold.   This is no exaggeration, he makes it look effortless.

Unfortunately we have not all got Neil's level of expertise. But is you really want to know how to execute the cross arm bar you can do know better than seek him out for instruction.

On the street though we should be aware that as always no matter how good we are at a certain hold we should not launch ourselves onto the floor just to apply it.

I recall a tale Mr. Gary Spiers related on one of his seminars. He said he had an Olympic standard wrestler working the 'door' with him in a nightclub. During the evening this guy had an altercation with a 'clubber'. The wrestler knocked this person to the floor and then fell into a cross arm bar holding the man there.   Later Gary Spiers said he terminated this wrestler's employment because he put himself at an un-necessary risk by going to the floor.

Mr. Spiers said in some countries he has worked somebody would come over to you and have shot you dead while you lay there! You can't argue with the view of a man who has been in front line security for more than 35 years. What he was trying to say, was the circumstances in which it was chosen to be used were in-appropriate.

Now if you do choose to use the cross arm bar in a real all out survival ground grappling encounter remember that your opponent isn't going to be tapping out and submit, you may well have to be mentally prepared to break an elbow to win the fight. Some guys pumped up with alcohol and drugs will be impervious to pain. They will struggle on and on and in some instants will fight on even if you break the arm! In some kind of competition or contest no matter how determine your opponent may be he will not want to risk a broken arm, 'outside' it may not be the case.

There takes a certain amount of mental resolve to break an arm. Most people will readily punch and kick somebody but 'taking and breaking a limb' requires some 'bottle'. It's like the person who prefers if he had to, to shoot somebody rather than stab them. There is something more personal about it. So be prepared if you are going to use the arm bar to have to take it to the limit and beyond, you must condition your mind for this event.

PRIME COMPONENTS FOR A GOOD CROSS ARMBAR

There are many ways of taking the cross arm bar. I am going to outline one of them and emphasize the important points that I think can give you success in applying this lock.

We are going to look at the lock from the 'mount' position. You are on the mount punching down onto your opponent, he begins to turn onto his side to protect against the punishment and pushes up with his hands to fend off your strikes. Let's say for example, he turns to his left. You bring up your right foot and tuck it tight into his ribs preventing him from rolling anymore. Now grab the 'crook' of his left elbow deeply with your forearm using your right arm. With your left push strongly down onto his jaw with the heel of your hand, bear your weight onto it and pivot off to your left sitting back to apply the cross arm bar. Have your butt tight to his shoulder.
Control crook of his arm, then let your left arm run up his forearm as you lie back and straighten his elbow. Pinch your knees firmly either side of his elbow; have his thumb facing upper most. Now lift your pelvis off the floor as you crank down on his arm to apply the arm bar. Make sure your legs are in a protected position to avoid a bite. Refer to photos.

Key Points

a) Control crook of his arm - This prevents him using the strong bicep and shoulder muscles to foil the hold. This will happen if you make the mistake of grabbing his wrist first.

b. Pin Jaw - This gives you a great point of control and stops him moving as you make the transition to the side.

c) Butt tight to shoulder - Sit down and not fall back into lock, again this keeps it all tight and gives no room for an escape.

d. Pinch Knees - Pinch your knees tightly either side of his elbow to under and in place for leverage.

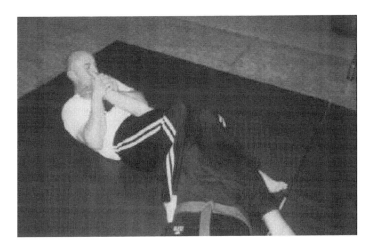

e. Thumb uppermost – His thumb must stay 'skywards' to have his elbow under and in place for leverage.

f. Lift Hips - Lifting the hips in conjunction with levering the arm down against your thigh gives you a powerful arm bar.

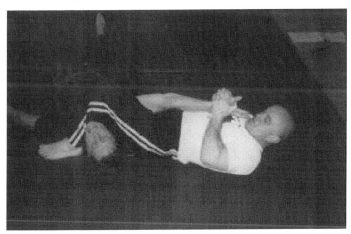

Breaking the 'catch' position

The 'catch' position is a grappling manoeuvre where your opponent will link up both of his hands tightly to prevent you straightening his arm out.

There are many different ways of countering this movement but for the sake of this text, where we want to get the 'job' done as quickly as possible we will look at a couple of basic but highly effective techniques.

Let's say you have your right arm in the crook of his right and pulling to break his grip. From here use your left hand in a downward hammer fist action and smash it into his nose for a release. If you are controlling his arm with your left, smash your right hammer fist into his solar plexus or groin. After both of these moves, if his arms are only just slackened, kick hard with the heel of your foot into the bicep of his far arm to break grip.

Now drive your heel again down into his bicep as you straighten his elbow on nearside arm for the cross arm bar/break. To get up safely from this position, drop a leg guillotine strike with your calf into his face. Next shuffle hip away, drive the heel of

your foot into the soft spot under the earlobe and then get up
quickly to your feet.

In closing this chapter, joint locks take a long time to perfect
correctly, you will have to drill them more than any other
technique on the floor and don't lose track of when and where to
execute them. When we talk about joint locks this will also
include the legs. Only in recent years have grapplers become
aware of attacking the legs. I learnt leg locks very early in my
Ju Jutsu training but it's not until in recent times arts like Sambo
and Shoot wrestling have brought them to the fore.

Leg locks are highly effective with constant drilling but again
you have to apply the same principles to them as mentioned with
other joint locks. 'Horses for courses', as they say!

On the following pages are a few examples of some very painful
locks on the legs. If you want to explore these type of moves
seek out a good instructor to teach you. Have a look at the
following. Are they practical for street grappling?

106

Chapter Ten

Devastating Anti Rape Techniques

Floor Fighting with 'BITE'

For most ladies in a rape or assault situation they will find themselves pinned down on the ground, bed, car seat, etc, etc. They will have to learn the majority of their fighting techniques from a recumbent position right away, usually they will not have the choice whether to fight standing up or take it to the floor. All ladies must know a handful of basic and brutal techniques to survive this nightmare of rape or abuse.

I have found through my experience of teaching ladies self protection is that it's no major problem getting them to learn the mechanics of a certain strike etc, it's getting them to believe they can do this in a 'real' situation and trying to help them over the infamous 'freeze' syndrome of shock and also getting them into the frame of mind to 'fight back'.

Most ladies would fight 'tooth and nail' to save one of their children from harm but will not do the same for themselves, believing that if they don't fight back in a rape situation then they won't be hurt. Wrong! There are no such guarantees and there are many documented cases of ladies who did not resist rape that still ended up battered, tortured or murdered.

This book is not really the place to deal with the psychological side of rape defence.

You should refer to Jamie 0'Keefe's *'Dogs don't know Kung Fu'* a guide to female protection for a first class view on this and many other relevant topics concerning ladies Self Protection.

This chapter is going to look at certain physical responses a lady can use to save her life and fight back effectively using realistic ground fighting methods.

The guard position that we looked at earlier is a classic rape position for a woman. She will have to use it to her advantage when she has no other choice left.

Wrap your legs tightly around your attacker and then using your leg strength pull attacker down towards you and thumb gouge his eyes, go in deep and look to maim, 'A blind man cannot fight back'!
Some women will say 'I couldn't do this '. You must remember, we are talking last-ditch survival here, if it's your life at stake what choice have you got, you will have to do it. Alternatively you can grab attacker's ears or hair and bite hard and deep into his neck or throat, clamp on and bite like a rabid dog to finish the job. You can then thrust your hips back pushing attacker away, shuffle back your hips and drive a foot into his face and get to your feet.

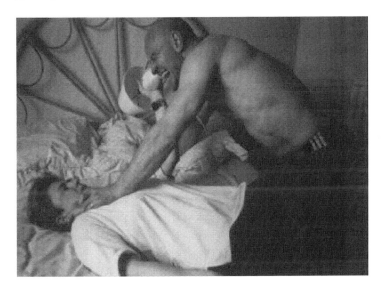

If the assault is on your bed use anything at hand to batter him with. Lf you have a phone on your bedside table use it, or a table lamp, ashtray, glass, whatever is available.

If attacker is straddling you or leaning over your body, suddenly drive a knee or shin up into his crotch or smash your head upwards into his face and then get off the bed.

If you are forced to fondle your attacker do so and when the opportunity is there, crush his testicles or bite hard to his genitals. Brutal but highly effectively!!

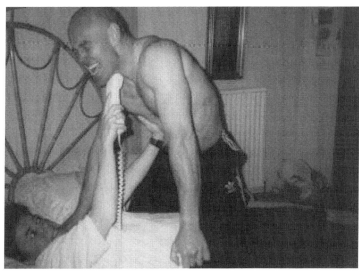

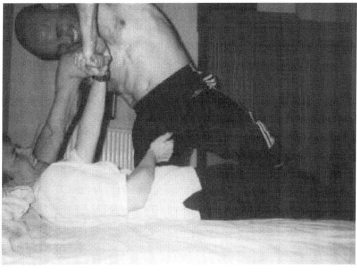

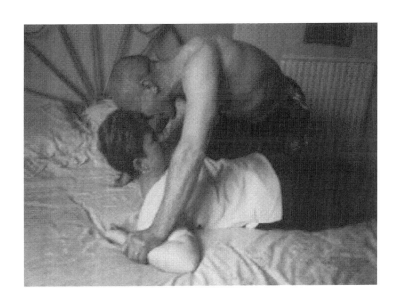

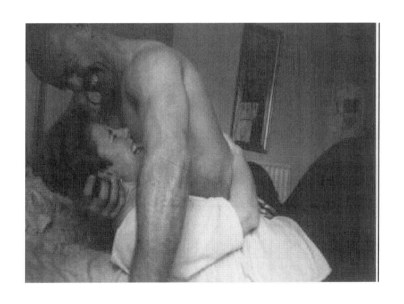

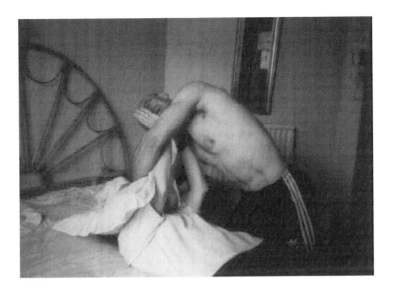

Remember there will be some opportunity to use these moves; it will all depend on your mental capacity to use them and your swiftness of mind.

Biting is essential and an opportunity will be there, anywhere bitten is painful. The neck/throat prime targets, nose, ears, lips, neck, genitals, and nipples also are main targets. It will give you positive results. If a hand is shoved over your mouth see if you can 'worm' the little finger into your mouth and bite down on it like a chicken bone for a release.

If you want to drill scenarios remember the soft and springy surface of a mattress on a bed is different to a harder floor surface. It is best to train on both surfaces.

The techniques and tactics outlined here are only a handful but they are guaranteed to have an instant effect on your attacker, if they don't incapacitate him, they will certainly give you a chance to regain your feet and look for an escape. Of course all this depends on your state of mind and readiness to fight back or more worrying your, conscious state if you were initially knocked to the floor. Teaching break-falls in a ladies self protection class may not be such a daft idea. Finally as always avoiding being 'down' is your priority in the first place.

Female of The Species is more deadly Than the Male !

Black Widow. One bite is fatal !

Chapter Eleven

'One up, one down!'

'What to do if you are on the floor and attacker is standing'

I feel this area should be addressed when we explore ground grappling for reality. It is an area often overlooked when floor fighting is discussed.
During an upright alteration you may well be pushed, shoved, tripped or punched to the floor and have your attacker looming over you. Alternatively you could have slipped on an icy pavement, beer soaked floor, off the edge of a kerb etc and found yourself suddenly on the 'deck'. Whichever way you will need to know what to do to save yourself from getting kicked to pieces!

Knowing how to fall correctly can go a long way to preventing hurting yourself initially when you go down. Judo and Ju Jutsu classes will teach you break-falls from your first lesson and it may well do you some good to get some practise in falling correctly. In my own Ju Jutsu classes we spend time getting people to fall safely on the mats and then progress them to grass, wooden floors and finally concrete. For practicality you must learn how to fall on a hard surface minimizing damage, falling on mats is not enough. I am not going to go into the dynamics of break falling in this book but it is well worth your time seeking out instruction in this particular topic.

When you hit the floor you will need to protect yourself immediately.lf you are on your back, draw your knees up and present the soles of both feet as a shield to ward off kicks and also to prevent the attacker getting past your legs. Now at any given time lash out kicks to the knees or shins of your opponent, if you make good contact at the very least it will buy you time to get to your feet again. Be careful never to get up off the floor face first, this is dangerous and inviting a kick in the face, check out photographs on how to get up safely

If your attacker attempts to straddle your legs, kick up into his groin, if he bends over to grab at your legs treat him to a mouthful of your boot!

Just keep moving and kicking, it is really extremely dangerous and difficult to get past a person trained to fight from this position. The Brazilian fighters are excellent at this and I have seen fighters fend off others for up to 15 minutes in this position. I have also seen on videotape Renzo Gracie knock out Oleg Taktarov with a kick to the face from this position in a N.H.B. fight.

But recognize from your point of view the longer you are in this position the more riskier it can be for you in case more than one person wants to take a kick at you. However time spent drilling in this position is time very well spent.

What if your attacker gets past your feet and takes a kick or stomp at your head? Firstly you have to tuck up tight.

Knees pulled up to protect groin and abdomen, forearms tightly wedged in front of your face. This position protects your most vital of targets from getting hit.

I am going to describe a couple of defence techniques that again are pretty straightforward and can be learnt in minimum time. As opponent kicks at your face, roll into the kick and smother it, taking the stifled force on the 'meaty' parts of your forearms. Never roll away from a kick; otherwise you will take the full force of it as the kick builds up impetus.

Now as an example lets say you block his right leg, you hook your right hand behind his heel and roll the full weight of your body into his knee, looking to snap the tendons and put him on his back, immediately follow up with strikes to any exposed targets.
This technique can also be performed against a head stomp. You just roll under the stomping foot and into his supporting leg, the same way, this will drop him very quickly and damage the knee.

Another method is to smother the kick, grab the ankle and bite into the Achilles tendon on the heel or sink your teeth into the calf muscle, this usually has an immediate and painful effect! As soon as attacker hits the floor follow up with blows and get to your feet. Usually he will fall onto his belly giving you a chance to get onto his back for a strangle or choke if you feel you have to fight it out on the floor.

As mentioned earlier you do not want to get up face first from the floor but maybe you have been dragged down to 'all fours' and your attacker stands up to launch a kick at your head. Again move in and smother the kick with a cushioned 'X' block with the fleshy inner forearms from here apply hard and fast double sandwiching punches to the nerve points on the outer and inner side of the leg just above the knee joint. This has a crippling effect and can collapse the leg, you can follow up with a leg takedown or uppercut punch into his testicles and then regain your feet.

These are a few suggestions and methods that I have found effective when we have the one up, one down scenario. Remember though they need drilling and sooner you are on your feet again the better.

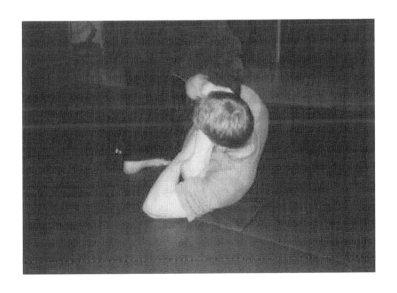

Before closing this chapter lets look at some of the best finishers when you get up and have your opponent flat on their back or belly.

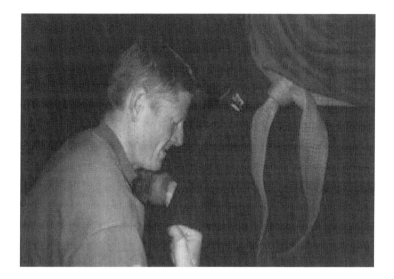

Opponent on back - Firstly you must know any kicking or stomping the head and neck area can lead to lethal results, you can kill people like this, you must be very very careful when and how you use this technique. Less lethal but highly effective finishers are knee dropping onto the ribs or chest, heel stomping the collarbone, ribs or solar plexus, stomping the groin/bladder and stomping onto the knees, ankles, elbows or hands. The last targets can stop somebody from getting up and giving chase or disarming of a weapon.

Opponent on belly - Knee drop neck, or between shoulder blades, heel kick spine or kidney. Stamp into the sciatic nerve in the middle of the thigh or stomp extremities again like arms and ankles.

'Opponent on all fours' - Kick in and up into the ribs, stomp onto his hands or Achilles heel. You can also use big downward elbows to his back/spine. Grabbing the hair or ears and kneeing the face is another option.

'You can't keep a good man down'

Chapter Twelve

'Fitness and Grappling'

'Can you last the distance?'

How fit do you need to be to grapple? Well if you are out of shape and inexperienced on the ground, 30 seconds of all out floor-fighting will seem like an eternity! If after 30 seconds to 1 minute you feel like your lungs are bursting and your arms and legs have become liquorice sticks, then you need to be fitter!

Please don't kid yourself that you don't need a certain level of fitness to fight on the floor even for a short duration, you will.

When it 'kicks off' the adrenalin will be pumping through your blood stream at a great rate of knots and your heart and lungs will be working overtime to accommodate your body with oxygen. You will go Anaerobic very quickly (this is working in great oxygen debt) because of the stress factor of a 'live' situation. The combination of all these things will drain your energy systems very quickly (Refer to my book **'In your face'** for a detailed explanation of the bodies energy systems and how they work under stress).
The fitter you are the longer you will last under these stress situations plus the more mentally prepared you are to deal with this stress factor the better you will cope.

As I have emphasised all throughout this book we want to finish the fight quickly and not let it become a long drawn out confrontation. But this may not always happen in the real world, so you have to prepare yourself.

You must at the very least be conditioned enough to last an all out 3 minute grapple on the floor. If you can do this you will be fit enough for most street encounters.

I have always been a bit of a fitness fanatic and as well as being a Martial Arts Instructor, I am also a fully qualified fitness coach and I believe in being 'fit to fight'. I want to be ready for any challenge if it suddenly happens. If you train for street self protection you are training for a confrontation that may happen in the next hour, next week, next month, next year, or never! it takes a great deal of will power and dedication to train day in day out but it has it's rewards, you will know at any given time you will have the stamina to last the pace in any situation.

There is no worst feeling than being pinned on the floor and your strength and stamina is rapidly fading away like bath water down a plughole! There is a saying that 'tiredness makes cowards of us all', and this is true. It's a nightmare feeling; you just want to curl up in a corner somewhere. But in

this situation you can't because you will have somebody pounding on you.

I have a thought that I always keep in my mind to motivate myself to train. It is, If I lose a fight it will not be down to my lack of 'conditioning'. I have trained myself to last out on a good day 30 minutes on the floor all out grappling! This takes some doing and for a street encounter, extreme, but the great feeling of confidence you can get from this is something special, So I feel everybody should be looking to last that little bit longer on the floor, even if your priority is to finish it as fast as you can.

Conditioning for grappling is specific and different to any other type of fitness training. You must develop good heart and lung strength through cardiovascular exercise and also good muscular endurance and strength not only in the muscles but the ligaments and tendons surrounding them. In grappling these take a lot of wear and tear and must be continuously strengthened.

I don't want to get too deeply into workouts and exercise but I will just give you a brief overview of what you might need.

Firstly though lets examine exactly what the body is going to feel when it hits 'grappling mode'. Recognize that as mentioned before street grappling and competition grappling will differ not only in its tactics but also how your bodies energy systems will work.

In a competition you will have ample time to warm up, stretch out and prepare your mind to do battle. You will know the rules that you will be fighting to and maybe even your opponent! You may have studied their strength and weaknesses. You will have trained months for this confrontation and will be 'on top of your game' and raring to go!.

Now lets examine a possible street scenario. You may have just finished an excellent meal in a restaurant with your partner. Shared a good bottle of wine or had a few beers and you are feeling relaxed and comfortable as you walk back to your car. Suddenly there is a guy in your face and before you know it he's swinging a blow, you clinch, wrestle and hit the hard wet pavement! A big difference. In this instance your body has to cope with switching on from 'cold' to mega 'hot' within seconds. No warm ups, no stretch, no time to gradually feel your way in, no anticipation, no knowledge of who your adversary is or what rules he's going to 'play' to.

A totally contrasting condition to the competition scenario. You will not be fighting in a time or place of your choosing, it will be thrust upon you. Remember an attack can happen anywhere, anytime, not always when you are feeling 'up for it'. Not when you have just finished training and are on a high. It could happen when you are feeling under the weather, carrying an injury, when you are cold, wet and tired and want to get home. This is when it's mentally tough to switch on and defend yourself, but if you are training in reality based 'street' Martial Arts this is what you have to consider. Some street predators will instinctively look for when you are at your most vulnerable. Staggering home at 2 a.m. after a 'session on the lager' is not sound self-protection and you are leaving yourself open for attack. Imagine having to grapple for your life in that state. Or grappling the next morning first thing with a massive hangover! It could well happen.

In the first moments of a grapple your body will react ferociously. Your blood pressure will soar up high and your heart and lungs will be working overtime, plus every muscle, tendon and fibre of your body will be under extreme stress. It's like starting up a car engine from cold and putting it into fifth gear and trying to get it to maximum performance, it will screech in protest, as it has not yet warmed up and got the engine oil circulating for smooth operating.

JUST LIKE YOUR BODY SYSTEM under STRESS!

The novice on the floor will use up all his energy rapidly. There will be so much tension in his muscles they will not be able to draw oxygen in and will fatigue quickly. Try now whilst sat reading this book to tense every muscle hard and see how long you can hold that position before you need to relax, you will then get the picture of what I'm talking about. Also they will have problems controlling their adrenalin and be gulping in mouthfuls of air like a fish out of water!
The veteran knows these feelings and will immediately, cope with them. He will know when to tense and when to relax his muscles, know when to snatch a breather and take in oxygen. He will be thinking all the time with icy aggression and purpose. Look at Master ground fighters like Royce and Rickson Gracie, their coolness and unruffled demeanour under pressure is something else, nothing seems to phase them or break their concentration, for them it's just 'another day' at the office!
The more you train your body under these stress circumstances, the more it will react in the right way. Apart from grappling you must find an exercise routine to simulate these conditions that bring you to an anaerobic state quickly. Peter Consterdine's book 'Fit to Fight' goes into this form of training excellently and is well worth a read.
I teach and work a method of exercises I call `THE BLITZ'. I will take an exercise and get people to work it for 60 seconds flat out, as many repetitions as possible, no slacking. You don't want to cruise your way through the minute; you have to push

yourself until you cannot squeeze another rep. Then have 20 seconds rest and pick another exercise and repeat.

You can do this with say 6 exercises up to 10 exercises depending on your fitness level. If you have done it correctly the 6 minutes will feel like 30 minutes! Your muscles should feel heavily fatigued and you may even feel nauseous. I have known certain individuals running for the toilets after a 10 minute 'BLITZ' session.

Here is an example of a 6-minute and 10 minute BLITZ.

6 minute BLITZ - 1 minute each exercise, 20-second rest between each exercise.

1) Burpee with a knee tuck up
2) Squat Thrust
3) Press ups
4) Jumping squats
5) Ab crunches
6) Alternating leg raises

10 minute BLITZ

1) Burpee with a knee tuck up
2) Jumping squats
3) Press ups
4) Star-jumps
5) Squat thrust
6) Vertical wall push ups
7) Neck Bridging
8) Ab crunches
9) Alternating leg raises
10) Close stance squats and jumps

Give them a try and see how you get on with them. Remember it can be any combinations, any exercises, just use what you want. When I used to work in a timber yard in the dinnertime break I used to train in a part of a warehouse myself and a few mates had gradually over the months turned into a bit of a training gym. One of the many BLITZ routines I worked on was to do 10 long arm chin ups, followed immediately by climbing a 15 foot rope 3 times, a minute hard continuous punching on the bag and then drop down and bang out 20 press ups. All done without any rest, then take a 30 second rest and do it again. 3 sets in total before moving on to say 30 minutes bag work. Some of the routines were boarding on the barbaric, add to this sub zero temperatures in the winter in an open fronted warehouse with the wind whistling up the Bristol docks and you had an extreme and daunting training environment.

These BLITZ type drills not only give you good anaerobic conditioning but also a great reserve of mental muscle. They are hard to make yourself do, particularly solo, you may need a good partner to spur you on, because they do stress the system but they perfectly simulate the feelings of live combat.

You can't do this type of training all the time because it places too much demand on the body but every now and then you should give your body a short, sharp shock with it.

We will now take a brief overview of other types of fitness, which can help you as a martial artist.

With the cardiovascular side of things I have found using a piece of equipment specific to your needs is a great bonus. A rowing machine or a cross trainer not only gives the heart and lungs a great workout but also works the top and lower body simultaneously. They give a great pull and push action with the arms that work specific muscle groups and tendons and also simulate the pulling and pushing involved in grappling.

The cross trainer is like a cross-country ski and you can programme in a manual flat level to keep a constant pace.

A hill programme of progressively bigger sets of hills or a random programme of any combination of hills.

Also you can change the levels of intensity. For example level one gives you a really fast and light pace, level twenty is like going through quick sand, both beneficial for grappling. How long you work on these pieces of kit are up to you but for explosive grappling, quality and intensity are more desirable than quantity and distance.

If you can't get to use these type of machines, running and swimming are excellent stand bys but of course the best conditioning for grappling is grappling and plenty of it!

Muscular endurance is of extreme importance. Muscular endurance is how long a muscle can work through a certain motion until fatigued. Strength is no good without muscular endurance. You will find strength can ebb away quickly, grips will weaken, muscles will seize and energy will sap. Muscular endurance will keep you going, just like the Duracell battery!
If you are working weights (machines or free weights) go for high repetitions and moderate weight. You want to get around 3 sets of 25 or 30 reps out of any given exercise, as a rough guide. Free form muscular endurance exercises come in the way of press ups, squats, jump tucks, burpees, squat thrust etc, going to failure, as mentioned earlier.

Core strength is also essential, but remember you are not going to lift weights like a bodybuilder. For grappling strength you need to work on basic and standard exercises with free weights or machines. Exercises like, dead lift, squats, leg press, chest/bench press, lat pull downs, shoulder press and chin ups.

All these exercises will give you a core strength, all over the body.
You need to work up to lifting heavy with low reps 4 to 6. Be careful though it is tough and demanding lifting towards your

maximum reps. Always seek out professional help in a gym before carrying out any exercise plan.

Neck strength is essential for grappling. Regular front and rear neck bridging can build up great power in this region, particularly good for fighting back against chokes or strangles.

Forearm and grip strength is also of great value. Lifting of any weights will improve your grip. Hanging from a chinning bar or similar will also do it, as will rope climbing which is very demanding on the grip. The old stand by of squeezing a squash ball or a piece of modelling clay are still first class and can be done sitting in front of a television.

As mentioned this is only a brief look at what you need in the way of fitness for grappling and it's down to you how far you want to pursue it.

If you are interested in this area you may want to check out my video's **IMPACT JU JUTSU VOL. 1 and 2** for a more in-depth look at specialised training and exercises for the combat arts.

'You can't fake endurance'

A few examples of Grappling based techniques

Back Stretching for Grappling

Explosive Pushups for Strength and Endurance

Neck Strength Essential

Back Flexibility, A Must

Muscular Endurance with Weights

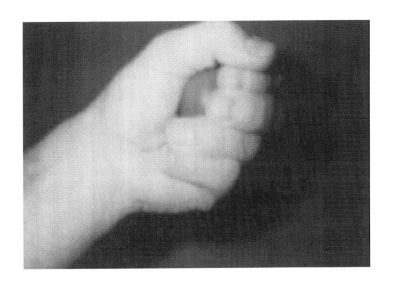

Squeezing a Squash ball for Forearm and grip strength

Working the pads from floor positions a definite conditioner

Chapter Thirteen

'Drills for street grappling'

'Practise makes Perfect'

The above saying is true but I think it would be even more clearer if it read lots and lots of practise makes perfect!!

All the things we have discussed and analysed in this book will mean nothing if you don't drill them and get in some good quality practise time.
Repetition may be boring but it's the only way to get things right.
Often if I'm in a bank or building society (no, not to do it over!) I wonder how the girls behind the counters can effortlessly work the computers. They just seem to go on autopilot and make it look so easy. If it was me doing it then the 24 hour banking system would be totally appropriate, it would take me that long!

Of course these girls are working these computers all the time that's why they are so good, the same has to go for grappling, if you want to get good on the floor! I personally feel I can never find enough time or be totally satisfied with the amount of time I get to work on the floor, I want to work more and try and reach that level of smoothness that I have seen from some world class grapplers. People like Rickson and Royce Gracie, Frank Shamrock, Eric Paulson and our own Neil Adams and Lee Hasdell I admire tremendously in the field of ground grappling.

To drill correctly on the ground you need to take first the pins and compliantly drill the move to get a feel, then add 50% resistance to learn about basing and transferring your weight. Next you can work up to l00% all out trying to maintain a certain pin and then swap from one to another.

You can then do the same with your finishes and your escapes, then mix it all in for all out grappling.

Remember for street grappling practise with light open fingered gloves so you can punch (under control) and use light touch elbows, knees and head butts plus touch biting and eye gouging. This makes your training as real as possible but you must also look after each other!

Grapple in Gi's, grapple in T shirts, grapple bare chested, all will be different. Also grappling with old street clothes to get a realistic feel. Grapple on mats, grass, wood and concrete, (wear enough clothing to protect yourself on hard surfaces).

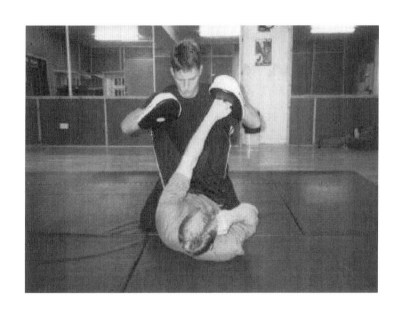

138

For solo work get a punch bag or large kick shield or if you can afford it a training dummy, put it on the floor and run through all your strikes and pins. This is a good work out as well as a super training drill for sharpening your striking tools on the floor.

With a partner you can strike the focus pads from mount, guard, 'knee on' and kneeling positions, another great drill for realistic training.

Try if you can to grapple with all types of partners. Get used to bigger and heavier opponents as well as light and 'nippy' ones, no two people are the same, they will all fight differently.

For a taste of real hell grapple 4 or 5 people in a row or grapple 2 people at a time or grapple an opponent armed with a knife. (rubber one please!) These things bring a new element of training to your floor work.

Also try grappling on a large crash mat, it's a great simulation to a bed mattress (remember you never know where you will be attacked). Lack of firmness and grip makes this drilling very difficult and demanding.

Again if you want more ideas for drills check out my IMPACT JU JUTSU VIDEO'S.

Try and be innovative with your training so you don't get stale and remember gear it to what you need and don't lose sight of your goals.

`TRAIN HARD-FIGHT EASIER'

quote from Peter Consterdine's excellent book 'Fit to Fight'

Chapter Fourteen

A personal insight to advanced ground grappling from the mat

In a street scenario I always believe going to the floor must be a last resort. 'Learn to fight on the floor but don't go to the floor to fight' is a smart motto. Sometimes though it cannot be avoided, you may be dragged down or lose your balance then you are forced to fight your way from the ground. When you do the tactics in this book and the techniques they should help you survive the encounter. As stated most people have no concept of skilled floor grappling but can still be dangerous if you don't heed the advice in this book.

As mentioned where you take your ground grappling and how far you want to delve into it will be your own personal choice. I have personally found it an Aladdin's Cave of treasures. A great big jigsaw puzzle full of pieces.
You start with one piece and then start adding to make up the complete picture. Remember though if it was a 1000 piece puzzle the first piece will be as important as the last because without either there will be something missing! However, once you have completed the puzzle, along comes a 2000 piece one and you start again! As you get used to the pieces you will then see how quickly you can assemble the picture.
You can also liken basic technique to writing the alphabet and advanced technique to doing joined up writing! You still basically have the same letters it's just that you are doing something different with them. If you experience an advanced ground grappler at work it can be inspirational and awe-inspiring to watch.

A few years back I went up to a Seminar in London, a multi-styled Seminar run by Peter Browne of Kempo Ju Jutsu Budo Association. One of the guest instructors was Franco Vacirea who now, I believe, is the first Brazilian Ju Jutsu Instructor teaching on a regular basis in the UK. Himself and his brother demonstrated and taught the art for most of the day and I spent most of my time on their mat.

Renzo Gracie in action

Myself and my fellow instructor Paul Flett with
Renzo Gracie and other Brazillian Instructors

Pictured after a BCA course in the company of
The great Neil Adams

At one point they gave a demonstration of what only could be described as playful ground sparring. This for me was truly inspirational. They both flowed effortlessly from one move to the next, counter to counter. They seemed joined together, their movement on the floor was something very special. They reminded me of a couple of big cats friendly fighting with each other, like they do. Graceful but also powerful.

I said to the guys who came with me that this was another level of fighting that we had not yet experienced. Even with many years ground experience, I felt I had just had a glimpse through a door that held many special secrets within.

When I got back to my own clubs I decided there and then that I must work on the idea of more movement and flow on the floor. Twelve months or so down the line with a lot of hard work I feel I have improved in big steps, although I also feel I have a long way to go before I could come close to what I had seen that day from Mr.Vacirca. But I believe that these drills of sparring about 50% all out are the key to improving your groundwork.

You see you are flowing and moving, experiencing many different ground positions, some you wouldn't put yourself in, in a live grapple. For example, turning on your belly is always a bad move in grappling but if you don't go there how will you know what it feels like, how you might survive it, or even escape?

When you learn floor work you will probably develop three or four pins, finishes etc, that you favour and will use time after time. In live grappling you will feel familiar and comfortable with them, but if you want to expand your repertoire, you will have to edge out of that familiar territory and drill new moves. With the flow drills you will experience lots of different positions some you won't like, but the more you work these the less fear they will hold for you.

To work the drills, just start with a partner kneeling and then work one for one on finishing holds. Wherever you finish, then your partner starts. Just roll around as if glued together swapping and exchange holds, etc, with about 50% resistance, so you still have to work a bit to achieve your finish. You can do this in rounds of two or three minutes or work up to one long round for endurance. I have worked with my training partner and good friend Paul Flett up to 40 minutes continuous. In that time you literally go through hundreds of positions and holds. A tremendous way to get your technique ingrained in your mind and also a test of mental and physical stamina. You can really begin to appreciate what these top class grapplers get up to when they are sparring on the floor for an hour or more at one time.

Every now and then you will need to test yourself with some all out ground grappling and also mixing it with strikes etc But on a daily basis 50% flow training is the best way to go because you don't pick up any niggling injuries like you do when you are regularly doing all out groundwork.

It's just the same as a boxer who spars 100s of rounds before a contest that is different to fighting 100s of rounds, he saves the real fight for the big occasion or he feels he is primed and ready at any time for the real thing.

There are many different floor drills that you can co-operate into your training, some of these are on my video's Impact Ju Jutsu. Training and conditioning for Combat!

Groundwork has a lot to do with sensitivity and being able to feel your opponent's every move, this takes a high level of training to achieve this, but the more time you spend on the ground drilling your moves the better that sensitivity becomes.

At the latter end of last year I attended a course run by the knock- down sport Budo Organisation. I met an instructor from Manchester named Mike Gregory, he was an experienced martial artist in many fields and he also had a vast knowledge of the arts. He was telling me he had practised Judo for many years and he went to train with a group of blind Judoists. He said that he didn't know what to expect or how to approach it. They were practising groundwork and he paired off with one of the group and within seconds he was pinned to the floor. This happened again and again, although these people had no sight, their touch and sensitivity was of a very high level and this made them phenomenal on the floor. You can see how this flow and sensitivity work is so essential, it was a great story. These attributes were also shown by Mr.Vacirca with his awesome display of Brazilian Ju Jutsu.

A student of mine recently was up in Scotland and went along to train with JKD specialist, Rick Young, who is also a great ground grappler. My student sparred with Rick on the floor and said he could not get past his guard, he said his legs just monitored his every move and countered him. He ended up greatly frustrated, as he just couldn't do anything with Rick. This is another example of that sensitivity and fine tuning needed to excel on the floor. If you watch any of the true Master grapplers their feet become another pair hands and have tremendous dexterity.

I also have been fortunate to share the mat with Neil Adams on a British Combat Association Seminar. This man's groundwork is phenomenal, he is working it in a class all of his own. During the last portion of the Seminar we all did some continuous back to back floor grappling and Neil joined in, without hardly breaking a sweat he arm locked countless people for fun, what a level of expertise.

Whilst writing this book l had the opportunity to get to train on a Seminar in Birmingham with Renzo Gracie well known Brazilian Ju jutsu and NHB fighter, also cousin of Royce and Rickson Gracie. What a great guy he was. He was extremely approachable and open in his teaching and had time for everyone. His level of grappling was Premier Division stuff.

His cool and unruffled technique under pressure was a lesson to be learnt.

I learnt much from sharing the mat with this true expert in his art.

Being in these peoples company and their like can spur you on to greater things. Mind you, you can go on all the Seminars you want and train with the greatest but you have got to take away knowledge and then drill and drill it in your own classes otherwise the knowledge is wasted. Hanging around these people alone will not make you a good grappler, practise will!

Some are born great, Some achieve greatness, and
Some have greatness thrust upon' em
W. Shakespeare.

Chapter Fifteen

Will the real Ju Jutsu 'stand up' please!

As mentioned at the start of this book grappling is mighty popular at present and particularly Ju Jutsu has enjoyed a rebirth. Some people see Ju Jutsu as the ultimate ground grappling art. There is no doubt Ju Jutsu can be highly effective on the floor and the majority of the techniques described in this book have been 'culled' from various forms of Ju Jutsu. But I feel it necessary to make the point that Ju Jutsu is a much more complete Art than only ground grappling. Most of the modern Ju Jutsu that is being practised on the floor is really Judo with may be a few variations. Real combat Ju Jutsu didn't encourage going to the floor if it could be avoided.

When I first started Ju Jutsu training in the earlier part of the 1980's floor work was just a small part of the overall picture. Standing strikes to vital points, joint breaks, chokes, sweeps and throws were the main arsenal of Ju Jutsu techniques. Usually finishing with one man on the floor and the other pinning him with a knee and then performing a joint break, submission or a finishing atemi strike. This ties in with the earlier theory of battlefield Ju Jutsu with warriors grappling in armour, you would not want to go to the floor otherwise it would have been difficult to regain your feet! Also considering you were in a mass of bodies wielding swords, spears and knives, falling to the ground would be suicidal.

Combat Ju Jutsu showed floor grappling but not to the extreme of today, where it is geared more to competition.

When I mention I am a 5th Dan in Ju Jutsu people automatically think I must be a master floor grappler, but for me most of my Ju Jutsu training over the years has been more complete and well rounded than just wrestling on the ground! 'True' Ju Jutsu is a complete art working in all fighting ranges with probably the widest syllabus of techniques in existence. It cannot be just pigeon holed into 'Oh that's floor grappling!'

I have in my time been privileged to train with some of the best instructors of Ju Jutsu in the world. Most of them in my opinion are in the UK. All have been different, all have put emphasis on different things, all had their own style and thoughts on how Ju Jutsu should be taught, but the one common thread they all have had is they could fight on their feet as well as the ground.

I feel I had to make this clear as some people who are just starting off in modern Ju Jutsu, be it Brazilian or whatever, please don't be misled into thinking floor grappling is all it is, also the techniques outlined in this book for ground fighting are more in line with how Ju Jutsu was really taught!

'People have just hit the idea of cross training, yet Ju Jutsu has been a hybrid art for as long as it has existed!'

Some Combat Jujutsu Finishes

154

Chapter Sixteen

A final 'grapple with reality'

Throughout this book, I have tried to give an honest and realistic view on how I see combat ground fighting. I hope it will help all who read this book to understand this area of self protection more clearly and objectively and not get the pavement arena and the mat area confused, the gulf can be ocean wide if you don't train correctly. To do this you have to be brutally honest with yourself and your methods of training. You will have to analyse your approach, philosophy and technique and begin to adjust it accordingly, not easy if you have been training in a certain way for many years! It's a lot easier to deny how 'it really is' and carry on in the old comfortable way. But deep down you will know you are kidding yourself and this can be a dangerous thing if reality comes knocking on your door.

Some people who do not really know me will assume I am a 'punch them out, head butt them and bite them' merchant, who has jumped on the self protection and grappling bandwagon. These people could not be more wrong.

I have never professed in any of my writing to being, a tough guy, doorman, body guard, ninja mutant turtle or super Kung Fu killer! What I am is a martial artist and one who has put 25 hard years of training in on the mats up and down the length and breadth of the UK. I've trained under some of the best instructors from the UK, Europe, Japan, USA and many more countries.

I have had a quest to find 'my truth' in the combat arts and it's been a long hard journey!

In that time I have trained in and experienced most arts not just Ju Jutsu in which I hold a 5th Dan black belt. I have always had an open mind to all arts and I am a realist that has tested his art and theories in the real world as well as the Dojo and has found himself.

Sure I can teach you how to knock out an opponent quickly or choke him senseless. I can show you how to deal with today's street thug but I can also show you 100's of techniques of classical Ju Jutsu and Aiki Jutsu.

I can box, kickbox, grapple, use weapons and hold my own in most arts. I am not a master of them all but I have not been afraid to try them.

'It's' what you don't understand that you fear most!

This is why I write my books to honestly educate those who are still on their journey, who are confused with the myriad of martial arts all claiming to be street effective and combat orientated. I write to genuinely help these people discover their 'truth'. When I am asked to teach on a seminar or at any class, I teach to try and pass on knowledge and hopefully give people something they can take away and use.

A lot of so called instructors demonstrate techniques on seminars to massage their own massive egos and to show 'how deadly' they are without one jot of concern whether a student can pick up a technique or even remotely grasp the concept. I could name some so called 'big guns' in martial arts that do this but that would be wrong. To me they are bullshitters, wrapped up in their own swaggering self-importance, who just take the 'money and run'; my advice is avoid these people like the plague.

When I eventually 'hang up my Gi', I want people to say of me, 'that guy practised what he preached and was genuine, he told it and taught it how it is'. Obviously not everybody will agree with that, but as long as I know inside then I will have achieved what I have worked hard for over many many years.

The truth is out there, now when you find it, it may not be everything you thought it would be. You have got to learn to handle it!

'I tore myself away from the safe comfort of certainties through my love for the truth and truth rewarded me'. **Quote.**

'The truth that makes men free is for the most part the truth which men prefer not to hear'. **Quote.**

DOOR OF OPPORTUNITY

Bristol Goshin Jutsu Combat Academy in Training

Drill for Skill

Practice Makes Perfect

Train up and Down !

The End ..

Adverts

Will the reader please note that the following advertising section of the book is included to let you know of other Self Protection related merchandise.

You the reader, have not been charged for the printing or paper used in this section. The cost for this has been absorbed by New Breed Publishing.

The price that you have paid for this publication is for the knowledge, information and advice given by Kevin O'Hagan throughout the rest of this book.

Thank you

Marc Kaylor

Email

mkaylor.newbreed@talk21.com

VIDEOS
TO
BUY

By

KEVIN O HAGAN

COMING SOON!!!!!!!
A new video from Kevin O Hagan
DOWN AND OUT Vol 2

More dynamic Strikes, throws and submission techniques.

Learn advanced combinations, joint locks, leg locks, chokes, strangles, and much more. This tape is loaded with first class technique.

Modern Combat Jujitsu at it s best

Price £15 inclusive of Post and Packing
Contact Kevin O'Hagan for more details.
Due out on release Jan/Feb 2000

"If I wanted to learn something new – this is the video that I would choose. In fact, Kevin O'Hagans videos are the most used tapes in my own personal collection. I have not released any videos of my own because I do not feel I could improve on Kevins instructional tapes!"

Jamie O'Keefe 5th Dan
'Hall of Fame Awardee 1999'
'Founder Fellow of the Society of Martial Arts'.

IMPACT JUJUTSU Vol 1

If you are serious about improving your
All round fighting skills and conditioning,
Then this video is for you.

Learn *Secret* skills for better striking,
Throwing and grappling
Plus many unique fitness and conditioning drills!

IMPACT JUJUTSU Vol 1
by
Kevin O Hagan, 5th Dan
(Kempo Goshin Jujutsu)

Learn dynamic drills, techniques and conditioning for realism
Through this combat Ju-Jutsu video.
Loaded with vital information
This tape is a must for anybody serious about training for peak
fitness and reality training skills.
Enjoy and learn from this informative and exciting new video
available **only** from Kevin O'Hagan.
Excellent value at **£ 14.00**
(*Please add £ 1.00 for postage and packing*)
Please make cheques payable to "**Kevin O Hagan**"
and post to
26 Alpine road, Easton, Bristol BS5 6BD

Telephone: 0117-9520248

"FISTFUL OF DYNAMITE"

**Yawara-Bo is an excellent and compact little weapon
That can be an instant source of painful control.**

**Anybody of any age can learn how to use this
Lethal little stick, quickly with good effect!**

BRISTOL GOSHIN JUTSU
COMBAT ACADEMY
PRESENTS

NEW VIDEO RELEASES FOR 2000

Featuring Kevin O'Hagan 5th Dan

FISTFUL OF DYNAMITE
YAWARA-BO TECHNIQUES

60 mins of dynamic techniques using this small but
highly effective weapon...plus substitute makeshift
Yawara-bo's from everyday articles...!

Excellent value at £ 14.00

(Please add £ 1.00 for postage and packing)

Please make cheques payable to "**Kevin O Hagan**"
and post to
**26 Alpine road, Easton, Bristol BS5 6BD
Telephone: 0117-9520248**

Genuine 60 minutes of action guaranteed

'Down & Out'

**Grappling and groundwork is the In thing
Within Martial arts at present.**

**If you want to expand your knowledge within this area,
this video is for you.**

**It s loaded with basic and advanced
throws and takedowns, with a
Multitude of ground submissions and finishes.**

"DOWN AND OUT"
STANDING TO FLOOR JU-JUTSU
TECHNIQUES

Featuring Kevin O'Hagan 5th Dan

"50" Throws and takedowns with a multitude of finishing holds and submissions!! Hard to find information and techniques on just one tape (60 mins)

Excellent value at **£ 14.00**

(*Please add £ 1.00 for postage and packing*)

Please make cheques payable to "**Kevin O Hagan**"
and post to
26 Alpine road, Easton, Bristol BS5 6BD
Telephone: 0117-9520248
Genuine 60 minutes of action guaranteed

IMPACT JUJUTSU Vol II

The follow on to 'Impact Jujutsu'

This time learn advanced drills, exercises and conditioning routines. Some unique to Kevin O Hagan and his Ju Jutsu system.

See it all put together in
Freestyle all out sparring too!

IMPACT JUJUTSU Vol II
The new follow up video to the successful
IMPACT JUJUTSU Vol 1

This time **Kevin O Hagan, 5th Dan Jujutsu,** and his senior instructor Paul Flett, take you through a full array of advanced exercises including:

Conditioning, Speed drills, Throws, Padwork, Groundwork drills, Boxing, Vale Tudo (Sparring) and much more…

This tape is a must for anybody serious about training for peak fitness and all round Cross training skills.

Enjoy and learn from this informative and exciting new video available **only** from Kevin O'Hagan.

Excellent value at £ 14.00
(Please add £ 1.00 for postage and packing)

Please make cheques payable to **"Kevin O'Hagan"**
and post to
26 Alpine road, Easton, Bristol BS5 6BD
Telephone: 0117-9520248

Book review by Geoff Thompson.
Grad. SMA. FSMA

I Thought You'd Be Bigger
A Small person's guide to fighting back.

Kevin O'Hagan is one of the up-and-coming stars of the martial arts in the Nineties. Author of many thought-provoking articles and now his first martial arts book, 'I thought You'd Be Bigger – A Small Person's Guide to Fighting Back' he is one of the highest ranked Ju-Jitsu players in the country today having recently acquired his 5th Dan. This book is a result of his life work in Ju-Jitsu and is a very worthy read for anyone, large or small, that is interested in bettering their chances of survival on the pavement arena.

You know, I've worked with violence and violent people all of my adult life and I've learned an awful lot about the human experience and the capacity that our species has to destroy its self over as little as a spilled drink in a bar or eye contact across a busy street: even minor traffic incidents these days seem to be justification enough, to some, to take the life of another human being-it is a hugely violent age that we find seem to find our selves in.

Because our problem on this spinning planet is large, one would automatically presume that it would take a person of equal proportion-i.e. very big- in the physical sense, to deal with or neutralise the problem.
Not so!

At least not from my experience. I have dealt with thousands of violent altercations, I have also had to deal with big men (the odd big woman too!) and faced many life threatening situations, because of this people, when they meet me for the first time, will invariably say in an almost disappointed tone **'Oh! I thought you'd be bigger.'**

What a great title for a book on self defence, if only Kevin O'Hagan hadn't thought of it first and beaten me to the post (Damn!)

Joking aside, it is a brilliant title for a book on self-defence and I can think of no man better qualified to write such a text as my good friend and colleague Kevin O'Hagan.

Not only is it a great title it is also a great book for anyone that thinks size, or lack there off, has any debilitating qualities when it comes to protecting your self and those that you love.

I can tell you categorically that the most ferocious fighters that I have ever worked with have been physically small, like Kevin, but absolute dynamite when the fuse was lit.

I have known Kevin for quite a few years now, not only is he a very personable man he is also a first rate martial artist, one of the few that I really admire and one of even fewer high graded martial artists in Britain that is not afraid to don the white belt and learn off just about anyone that has something of worth to teach.

He is a realist, one of the leaders in the new age of realism, he talks the talk and he walks the walk so I heartily recommend and endorse this text to anyone, of any size or stature, that wants to be better prepared when the metaphoric 'big bad wolf tries to blow your house down.

This is a great book, buy, read it and be bigger for the experience.

Geoff Thompson, Coventry 1998.

I THOUGHT
You'd be
BIGGER !

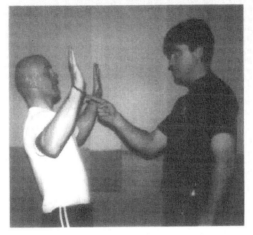

A SMALL PERSONS
guide to
FIGHTING BACK
by Kevin O'Hagan

Ever feel inferior or intimidated by a large person?
Maybe you have been bullied by such a person?
Maybe you have been the victim of violence 'offered' by a big aggressive assailant?
Or maybe you just live in fear of being attacked by someone bigger than yourself?
Our society has conditioned us to think BIG is strong and dangerous and small is weak, defenceless...
Time to re-think, the small person can fight back and win!
In "I thought you'd be bigger", find out the crucial mental and physical elements needed to survive a violent encounter with the 'big guy.'
Kevin O'Hagan a 5th Dan black belt in Ju Jutsu, gives you his valuable insights from *22 years experience of the Combat Arts* on this essential but over-looked topic in the world of the fighting Arts.
This book contains much sought after and hard to find information on personal self-protection for the 'little people.'
A real lifesaver!

ISBN 0 9517567 7 X

£12.99

New Breed Publishing
P.O.Box 511
Dagenham
Essex RM8 3NF
England

ISBN 0-9517567-7-X

9 780951 756775

Description - Book title	Unit Price	Copies	Total
I thought you'd be bigger- Book	£14		£
In your face-Book	£14		£
Impact JuJutsu Vol 1 (Video)	£15		£
Impact JuJutsu Vol II (Video)	£15		£
Fistful of dynamite (Video)	£15		£
Down and out (Video)	£15		£

I thought you'd be bigger
The small persons guide to fighting back
Written by Kevin O Hagan -   £14 inc P&P

In your face
Close quarter fighting
Written by Kevin O Hagan -   £14 inc P&P

Impact JuJutsu Vol 1
Training and conditioning for combat
Instructed by Kevin O Hagan -   £15 inc P&P

Impact JuJutsu Vol II
A full array of advanced exercises for combat conditioning
Instructed by Kevin O Hagan -   £15 inc P&P

Fistful of dynamite
dynamic techniques using this small but highly effective weapon
Instructed by Kevin O Hagan -   £15 inc P&P

Down and out
Standing to floor Ju-Jutsu techniques
Instructed by Kevin O Hagan -   £15 inc P&P

Please make Cheque/Postal orders payable to
"Kevin O Hagan"
And post to
26 Alpine Road, Easton, Bristol B55 6BD

If you enjoyed this book why not order the other titles currently available from Jamie O Keefe And Kevin O Hagan

THEY ARE AN IDEAL PRESENT
IF YOU WANT TO
GIVE SOMETHING DIFFERENT AND SPECIAL
If you borrowed this book
Why not get your
own copy!

In Your Face
'CLOSE QUARTER FIGHTING'
by
Kevin O'Hagan

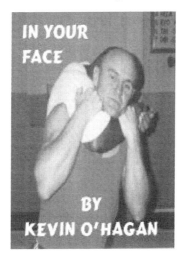

£14

from
NEW BREED
Or even better
Buy it direct from Kevin O Hagan
And ask him to autograph it!

Your Advert, Book, Video or Company
could be featured here
plus in our other books

Other books that are a must
For your collection

Read about the 20th Century
'Secret - self protection weapon'
also
Everything you need to know about
EDGED WEAPONS
in
'Dogs don't know Kung fu'
By Jamie O Keefe

THE BEST BOOK EVER WRITTEN
PREVENT YOURSELF FROM BECOMING A VICTIM
Dogs don t know Kung Fu

A guide to Female Self Protection
By Jamie O Keefe **£14** inclusive P&p

Never before has Female Self Protection used this innovative approach to pose questions like. Why do Rapist's Rape? Why are Women abused? Why do Stalkers Stalk? This book takes a look at all Simple, Serious, and Life threatening aspects of Self Protection that concern us daily, along with **PREVENTION** of Child abuse and Child Abduction, Emotional cruelty, Telephone abuse, Road rage, Muggers, Date rape, Weapon attacks, Female abduction, Sexual Assault & Rape, Self defence law, and what it will allow us to do to protect ourselves, plus much more. With over 46,500 words, 77 pictures and 200 printed pages "Dog's Don't Know Kung fu" is a no nonsense approach to women's self defence. It covers many realistic scenarios involving Children's abduction as well as typical attacks on women. Besides quoting actual events, the book explains how to avoid trouble and how you should react if you get into a situation.

This book is a must read for all women and parents.
It is also important for teenage women, but, due to some of its graphic depiction's of certain incidences, parents should read it first and decide if it's suitable for their child.

What Makes Tough Guys Tough?
The Secret Domain

WHAT MAKES

TOUGH GUYS
TOUGH
The Secret Domain
by Jamie O'Keefe

Written by Jamie O Keefe

Jamie O'Keefe has interviewed key figures from Boxing, Martial arts, Self Protection, Bodyguards, Doorwork, Military, Streetfighting and so on. Asking questions that others were too polite to ask but secretly wanted to know the answers.

Interviews include **Peter Consterdine, Geoff Thompson, and Dave Turton** from the countries leading Self Protection organisation "The British Combat Association".

Along with Boxing heroes **Dave 'Boy' Green** and East London's former Commonwealth Champion **Mo Hussein**.

Plus unsung heroes from the world of Bouncers, Foreign Legion, Streetfighters, and more.

This book also exposes the Secret Domain, which answers the question "What makes tough guys tough".

Find out what some of the toughest guys on the planet have to say about "What makes tough guys tough" and how they would turn you into a tough guy.

Thugs, Mugs and Violence

In this true account of his journey, Jamie O'Keefe unveils the reality of living in the East End of London. From childhood to adult this compelling, harrowing and often highly amusing story tells of his encounters with streetfighting, crime, drugs, violence and the martial arts. It goes through the trials and tribulations of boyhood right through to his days of working on the door in the heart of London's nightlife. Read how each of his confrontations and experiences have played a major part in making him the well respected authority in the fighting arts that he is today.

This book is sure to intrigue and fascinate you so much it will be hard to put it down..

"Jamie's book 'Thugs, Mugs and violence' is an insight into the violent times of today and should be read" **Reg Kray 'Kray Twins'**

Photograph kindly supplied to Jamie for inclusion by

**REG KRAY
31 YEARS
SERVED
1968   1999
HM Prison.**

THUGS, MUGS
and
VIOLENCE

An Autobiography
By
Jamie O'Keefe

One mans encounter with Thugs, Mugs and Violence
as a Bouncer, Martial Artist, Streetfighter and former
East end gang member.
A fascinating book that will introduce you to
Life's hidden world of drugs, guns, violence,
and revenge.

£14 inc p&p
from NEW BREED
Po box 511, Dagenham Essex RM9 5DN

THUGS, MUGS
and
VIOLENCE

REVIEWED AS
'BOOK OF THE MONTH'
Front magazine

£14 inc p&p
from NEW BREED
Po box 511, Dagenham Essex RM9 5DN

How would you like to be able to
Stop an attack in its tracks?

How would you also like to be able to do it
within a second or two?

How would you like to do it without even
having to draw a breath?

Finally, would you like to know what the
alternative to grappling is?

Then get

"Pre-emptive strikes for winning fights"
"The alternative to grappling"

by
Jamie O Keefe

Pre-emptive strikes

for winning fights
"The alternative to grappling"

by
Jamie O'Keefe
£ 14 inc P&P
from
New Breed
Po Box 511
Dagenham, Essex RM9 5DN

Description - Book title	Unit Price	Copies	Total
Dogs don t know kung fu	£14.00		£
Old School, New School	£14.00		£
What makes Tough guys Tough	£14.00		£
Thugs, mugs, and violence	£14.00		£
I thought you'd be bigger	£14.00		£
In your face-Book	£14.00		£
Pre-emptive strikes **For winning fights**	£14.00		£

Dogs don t know kung fu
A guide to Female Self Protection
Written by Jamie O'Keefe - £14.00 inc P&P

Old School, New School
A guide to Bouncers, Security & Door Supervisors
Written by Jamie O'Keefe - £14.00 inc P&P

What makes Tough guys Tough
The Secret domain
Written by Jamie O'Keefe - £14.00 inc P&P

Pre-emptive strikes for winning fights
The alternative to street grappling
Written by Jamie O'Keefe - £14.00 inc P&P

I thought you'd be bigger
The small persons guide to fighting back
Written by Kevin O Hagan - £14.00 inc P&P

In your face
Close quarter fighting
Written by Kevin O Hagan - £14.00 inc P&P

NEW BREED Po box 511, Dagenham, Essex RM9 5DN

If you enjoyed this book why not order the other titles currently available from

Jamie O'Keefe
And
Kevin O'Hagan

THEY ARE AN IDEAL PRESENT
IF YOU WANT TO
GIVE SOMETHING DIFFERENT AND SPECIAL

If you borrowed this book and would like your
own copy, give
Kevin O'Hagan a call on
0117 9520248

(Get Kevin to sign and personalise your copy)

Your Advert, Book, Video or Company
could be featured here
plus in our other books

Our books make ideal unique

Christmas
And
Birthday
Gifts

Be different and give something
That will remain with them for life

NEW BREED BOOKS

**Would you like to write a book
or become an author?**

NEW BREED PUBLISHING
Turned this book idea into reality
For Kevin O'Hagan

If you have an idea for a book and would like
to see it in print

Write to us to see if we can help you out.

- Please do not send us any manuscripts or
ideas without prior arrangement

**Contact New Breed Publishing
At
PO Box 511
Dagenham
Essex
RM9 5DN**

NEW BREED PUBLISHING

- Do you want to advertise in our books?
- Do you want to become an outlet for our books?
- Do you want to become an agent for us?
- Do you want to join our mailing list?
- Do you want to organise a course or Seminar with one of our Authors?
- Do you want to speak to or meet one of our Authors?

We can work together!

Contact Marc Kaylor

At New Breed Publishing

by writing to

**New Breed
Po box 511
Dagenham
Essex RM9 5DN
England**

Or via Email

mkaylor.newbreed@talk21.com

Would you like to train to be a Door Supervisor?

We are the only training company recommended by NEW BREED and run courses for Jamie O'Keefe on a monthly basis.

If you would like to attend one of our courses approved by Westminster, Kent and Dacorum to becoming a licensed door supervisor please give us a call to discuss your requirements.

Our courses are held in Central London but we can also arrange for them to be held at your location either in the U.K. or overseas.

If you read and enjoyed the Jamie O'Keefe book
'Old School – New school'
Then our course will suit you.

For further information please call **A.S.P. Security & Training**

On 0181-473 2084

Or write to

A.S.P.
36 Mottisfont road
Abbey Wood
London
SE2 9LN

* Please mention where you saw this advert

The latest book by Jamie O Keefe
Due out in the year 2000

"At The Sharp End"

A guide to self-protection against Edged Weapons

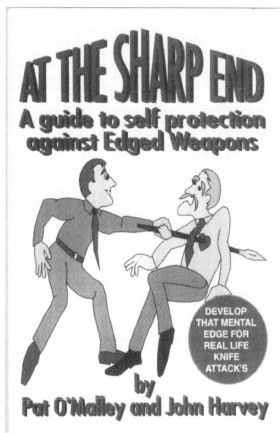

By
Pat O'Malley & John Harvey
£ 14 including Post and Packing
from
New Breed
Po box 511, Dagenham
Essex RM9 5DN

"Rapid Arnis Training Video"
Philipino Art of Self Defence

By
Pat O'Malley
World stick fighting champion 1998
£ 21 including Post and Packing
from
New Breed
Po box 511, Dagenham
Essex RM9 5DN

Do you have access to the Internet?
If so   why not write a review on this book

Go to

www.amazon.co.uk

Under <u>authors</u> search for
Jamie O Keefe or Kevin O Hagan

Then type in your review or comments
about any of Jamie's or Kevin's books
for the whole world to see!

Tip: Write up your review before you go
on line - then cut and paste your review,
which will make a great saving on your
phone bill

To let us know about the review you
submitted so that we can write back and
personally thank you!

VIDEO MAGAZINE

Video No2 features an interview
With Jamie O'Keefe
About his books
Available from
Martial Arts Illustrated
Telephone 01484 435011 for price and ordering details
*Note: This is **not** Jamie's forthcoming
'Pre-emptive strike video'
* Please mention where you saw this advert

Would you like to get your next New Breed book from
NEW BREED PUBLISHING
FREE OF CHARGE!

Review any of our books and get your review published in any National Magazine and to show our appreciation we will send you your next book, of your choice absolutely free...

Before you buy another book!
Let us buy it for you!
It does not matter
Who the Author is!
Which Publishing Company!
or
The cost of the book.....
'AS LONG AS ITS NOT US'
(Jamie O'Keefe, Kevin O'Hagan or New Breed)
Write down the title of the book
The name of the Author
The price of the book
along with your
Name and address
Each week we randomly select a postcard and purchase
that chosen book for that person
All it cost you is a stamp and a postcard!
Send it in to
NEW BREED 'FREE BOOK' OFFER
PO BOX 511
DAGENHAM
ESSEX
RM9 5DN
**This free book offer is only for books not sold or
published by New Breed Publishing!*